ROGUES, REBELS, AND REFORMERS

Rogues, Rebels, and Reformers
A Political History of Urban Crime and Conflict

TED ROBERT GURR

in collaboration with

Peter N. Grabosky
Richard C. Hula
Louis H. Masotti
David Peirce
Leif Persson
Sven Sperlings

SAGE Publications / Beverly Hills / London

For information address:

SAGE PUBLICATIONS, INC.
275 South Beverly Drive
Beverly Hills, California 90212

SAGE PUBLICATIONS LTD
St George's House / 44 Hatton Garden
London EC1N 8ER

Printed in the United States of America

Library of Congress Cataloging in Publication Data

Gurr, Ted Robert, 1936-
    Rogues, rebels, and reformers.

    Includes index.
    1. Crime and criminals—Case studies. 2. Offenses against public safety—Case studies. 3. Criminal justice, Administration of—Case studies. 4. Crime prevention—Case studies. I. Title.
HV6251.G87   364'.9173'2   76-17370
ISBN 0-8039-0681-1

FIRST PRINTING

77-2273

CONTENTS

To my parents

Preface

This book sets out the conceptual foundations and comparative conclusions of a historical study of crime and conflict in four of the world's principal cities between 1800 and the present. The case studies of these cities—London, Stockholm, Sydney, and Calcutta—are published in a larger volume by Ted Robert Gurr, Peter N. Grabosky, and Richard C. Hula: *The Politics of Crime and Conflict: A Comparative History of Four Cities* (Beverly Hills, Calif. and London: Sage Publications, 1977). They contain detailed evidence to support most of the generalizations offered here. Our conclusions about the sources and consequences of public disorder merit publication in this form because their applicability extends far beyond the four cities investigated. We also wanted to make the conclusions available to students and other readers whose patience and pocketbooks might be exhausted by the unabridged edition.

We are particularly concerned about the interdependence between crime and conflict and the policies and institutions by which public order is defined and established—hence "the politics of crime and conflict." The ultimate aim is to provide a better understanding of what lies behind the apparent decline of public order in almost all the large cities of the West. The historical and comparative data are not likely to satisfy those who want answers to the immediate, practical question of what kinds of policies "work," because the measures that were effective prove to have been very different from one time to another. One of many conclusions not fully anticipated at the outset of this study is that public order depends more on basic socioeconomic and political circumstances than on conditions controlled by the law, the police, the courts, or the prisons.

We offer here a general description and interpretation of subjects usually studied separately and in narrower compass. The principal method is conventional historiography, but the coverage is inevitably superficial by most historians' standards because we have chosen to survey four societies over nearly two centuries. The concepts and hypotheses are mainly those of comparative political science, with particular reference to elites and contending class interests. The subject matter is traditionally that of sociology and criminology. By strict disciplinary standards, the study no doubt resembles one of those odd creatures portrayed in medieval bestiaries, part fish, part fowl, and part beast. We hope that it will be accepted as a contribution to a new, or at least rare, species of interdisciplinary study in which historical materials are used comparatively to formulate and test general theories germane to critical social issues.

A multiplying clan of social theorists has taken up the critical examination of ideological biases and unexamined premises in the empirical and theoretical scholarship of others. We shall be explicit about the values that inform this study. The principal contributors to this study prefer social order, however defined by the ordinary people of the societies we examined, to disorder. We have varying degrees of skepticism, though, about whether public order as defined and policed by governing elites has coincided with popular views. As the first line of social defense, we prefer tolerant, humanitarian policies, that is, conciliation and accommodation as the preferred methods of conflict management, and the avoidance of brutalizing punishment when dealing with offenders. We also recognize that in some social circumstances, humanitarian policies are not wholly effective or popular. None of us, though, advocates solutions of the kinds advocated on the extreme left or extreme right. One reason is the principled conviction that a substantial level of disorder is more tolerable than the annihilation of civil liberties in the service of revolution or reaction. The other reason is the skeptical conclusion, borne out by the results of this study, that draconian policies are no more certain to ensure public order than are humanitarian approaches. When faced with a choice between liberal policies that do not work very well and authoritarian solutions that have no better prospect of working, we much prefer the liberal alternatives.

The idea for a comparative historical study such as this was first advanced in 1971 by Prof. Marvin Wolfgang of the University of Pennsylvania and Drs. George Weber and Saleem Shah of the Center for Studies of Crime and Delinquency. The strategy of the study, including its general approach and the focus on urban crime and conflict, was devised by the senior author in collaboration with Prof. Louis H. Masotti, director of the Center for Urban Affairs at Northwestern University. The study subsequently was funded by the National Institute of Mental Health in all but its final phase, from 1972 through 1975. The senior author completed work on the manuscript in 1976 while supported by a Common Problems Senior Fellowship awarded by the German Marshall Fund of the United States.

The collaboration that produced this study requires a word of explanation. Peter N. Grabosky, Richard C. Hula, and David Peirce were appointed as research fellows of the Center for Urban Affairs and assumed primary responsibility for the studies of Sydney, Calcutta, and London, respectively. Prof. Masotti provided advice and administrative oversight for the project during most of its lifespan. Background papers on Stockholm were prepared on subcontract with the Institute of Criminology of the University of Stockholm by Leif Persson, Sven Sperlings, and a number of their students. Later Prof. Grabosky added to these papers and synthesized them. I prepared the conceptual framework of the study and carried out the comparative analysis, supervising and in some instances contributing to the city studies as well. All the Western cities were visited at least once and usually several times in the course of research. Although unavoidable political circumstances prevented us from doing field work in Calcutta, we had invaluable advice from Ramkrishna Mukherjee, Research Professor of Sociology at the Indian Statistical Institute, Calcutta. Of course, Prof. Mukherjee bears no responsibility for our conclusions about his native city.

Some of the qualities but none of the liabilities of this work are due to the advice and criticisms of other scholars, whom we thank. The theoretical and comparative sections of the work have been scrutinized in whole or part by Wesley Skogan and Frederick DuBow of Northwestern University, Neal Milner of Northwestern and the University of Hawaii, and Richard Rose of Strathclyde University, Scotland. The study of Calcutta was read with close critical attention by David H. Bayley of the University of Denver and John McLane of Northwestern, as well as by Prof. Mukherjee. Among the Australian scholars who aided the project, we would like particularly to thank Greg Woods and Gordon Hawkins of the Sydney University Law School. For comments on the Stockholm manuscript, thanks are due to Karsten Astrom, Leif Lenke, Ingemar Rexed, and Hanns von Hofer of the Institute of Criminology at the University of Stockholm. The London manuscript was evaluated by David Thomas and Nigel D. Walker of the Institute of Criminology, University of Cambridge. Inevitably during this close collaboration, the contributors often reviewed one another's findings and reinforced one another's interpretations; thus we have only ourselves to blame for the errors and perversities that critics will no doubt find.

This study has also relied on the talents and sustained labors of a number of people whose names appear nowhere else in the book. Tina Peterson was responsible for managing and analyzing the enormous archive of data we compiled on crime. The indicators of crime and the correlation analyses are principally her work, and she also contributed a background paper surveying other quantitative historical studies of crime. For more than two years Virginia Nicodemus managed the project's multifarious fiscal and clerical business, aided and abetted by Gaye Haverkos and Katherine Dolan. Erika Gurr constructed nearly one hundred graphs and tracked down many an obscure source and reference. A background paper by Mark Wynn reviewed for us some of the contemporary sociological and criminological literature on the definitions and causes of crime. Michael Stohl made available a collection of data on civil conflict in London. A number of others, students and secretaries, graphic artists and computer technicians, and many patient librarians at institutions scattered half-way around the globe, have given a helping hand to this enterprise. We thank them all. A special word of acknowledgement deservedly goes to our publisher, Sara Miller McCune, for making it possible to bring the study out quickly and in several different editions, the better to reach its potential audience.

Ted Robert Gurr
Cambridge, England
March 1976

PART I

PROBLEMS AND POLICIES OF

URBAN PUBLIC ORDER

Chapter 1

INTRODUCTION TO THE COMPARATIVE STUDY OF URBAN PUBLIC ORDER

Western civilization is centered on its cities, and Western people have come to judge their collective progress and well-being not only by their material and cultural accomplishments but by the civility and security of urban life. Reformers and social historians alike have celebrated the diminution of violence, venality, robbery, and riot in the nineteenth and early twentieth century histories of most European cities. North Americans have had fewer grounds for self-congratulation, but by and large they have accepted the European view that the citizens of the "good city" are as orderly as its municipal parks and public buildings. In the past generation, however, such optimism has been badly shaken by an apparent renaissance of disorder. By whatever indices one chooses—crime statistics or journalistic accounts, sociological treatises or public outcry—there has been a pronounced increase in crime and strife in most large Western cities. The phenomenon is by no means confined to Western cities either, though people of the world's poorer regions seem to be less alarmed perhaps because they have not thought themselves quite so close to the gates of the heavenly city.

To present a comparative history of urban public order, we describe problems of public order in London, Stockholm, Sydney, and Calcutta during the past century and a half, with particular attention to the evolution of the public policies and institutions that define and control disorder. These four cities were chosen partly because of their diverse cultural, demographic, and developmental traits, but mainly because each presents distinctive problems of public order. London, resting on Roman and Anglo-Saxon foundations, has the longest tradition of urban civilization. It is the largest of the four, and has led a double life: In the first half of the nineteenth century it was reputedly noisome and turbulent, ridden with vice and crime; yet by the end of the Victorian era it was known as one of the most civil and orderly cities of Europe. London thus poses two particular questions. One involves the extent to which the objective evidence either supports the conventional historical view (that the city became more orderly in the nineteenth century) or justifies the contemporary fear of rising disorder. The other asks whether it is possible to identify the altered circumstances and policies that contributed to the establishment of public order in the last century and the apparent renaissance of disorder in recent decades.

Stockholm, a smaller and newer city, is included as much because of its contemporary characteristics as for its historical background. Swedish society is notably prosperous, homogeneous, and egalitarian. The courts and penal institutions of Sweden have been leaders in innovative sentencing and rehabilitation practices. Politically the Swedish working class has been an effective, usually dominant political force since the 1920s. According to many theories of the etiology of disorder, these conditions should make contemporary Stockholm an exceptionally orderly city. The more problematic issue, though, is whether and how social programs and disorder have been linked over time. Did the incidence of crime in Stockholm decline in response to improving social conditions, or was it relatively low at the outset? Has institutional innovation contributed to the alleviation of crime, or was the low level of crime a precondition for official experimentation?

The two remaining cities in the study share legal systems and institutions of public order that derive from the English tradition but have virtually nothing else in common. Sydney was founded as a penal colony at the edge of a howling antipodean wilderness in 1788. Its problems as well as policies of public order were imported, so to speak, but after those rough beginnings we can trace in Sydney the evolution of distinctive patterns of criminality and public response to them. Sydney, like the new cities of North America, can be thought of as a vast social experiment. The opportunity existed to create a civil and orderly urban society, equipped with great resources and constrained by little except the cultural baggage of its citizens. The questions concern whether and how Sydneysiders have dealt with, and avoided, the problems of disorder that have beset most of the cities of Europe and North America.

Calcutta was chosen because it is so fundamentally dissimilar in history and prospects from the three Western cities; it does not typify Third World cities. A good case can be made that Calcutta, of the major cities of the world, has been least favored by circumstance. It was founded on a pestilent swamp by foreigners bent on exploiting

Bengal's wealth, and for nearly three centuries it served as a conduit through which that wealth was exported. In the twentieth century it has been swelled by a surplus rural population and waves of refugees who have far exceeded the city's waning economic opportunities and have overwhelmed its limited capacity to provide urban services. It has been wracked by famine, protracted revolutionary warfare, and chronic communal rioting. If one takes a pessimistic view of the urban prospect, one can paraphrase a remark made by Mayor Kenneth Gibson of Newark about American cities: Wherever the cities of the world are going, Calcutta will get there first. Yet Calcutta survives; somehow its people and rulers have evolved ways of living with endemic problems of public order.

We do not necessarily promise to answer all these specific questions because they may prove intractable. Nonetheless they dictated our choice of cities, influenced the kinds of information we sought, and suggested some kinds of analyses and interpretations of that information.

This study also has objectives that extend well beyond the ideographic analysis of public order in four cities. One general issue is whether there is historical warrant for the common scholarly and official view that crime and civil strife regularly declined in the nineteenth century in Western cities, then increased on some relative scale in mid-twentieth century. We assume that such a pattern exists as a working hypothesis for the three Western cities in the study; there is no conventional wisdom that would lead us to expect to find the same circumstances in Calcutta. It will be equally interesting to determine whether these trends—if they exist at all—are characteristic of all types of disorder, or only of some. This issue also stimulates us to ask whether there are distinctive patterns of change in disorder. We assume that changes have not been random, but there are three different ways in which systematic change could have taken place. One is that the incidence of disorder has changed gradually and continuously. The second is that changes have been abrupt and discontinuous but nonetheless cumulative. The last is that change is episodic, comprising recurring waves of rising and declining disorder. No one pattern of change will be universal. We want to know which patterns are characteristic of which kinds of crime and strife, at which times and in which societies. Particularly, have any of the cities experienced historically any great short-run increases in common crime that are analogous, in magnitude or character, to the apparent rise in crime since 1950?

The second general objective is to assess the relative importance of political and institutional factors in the creation and maintenance of public order. Crime and civil strife do not occur in a political vacuum. Both are defined by elites, with varying degrees of reference to or disregard of the views of other classes. Formally, the prevailing definitions of disorder encompass actions that are legally proscribed. In practice, disorder consists of actions that are resented and reported by citizens, policed by law enforcement agencies, and prosecuted and sanctioned by courts and penal institutions. One cannot understand the trends and patterns of criminality or strife without examining this institutional context. Therefore we want to identify major changes in the interests of rulers, legal codes, police systems and operations, and judicial and penal procedures. Suppose now that we do find distinctive patterns of change in policies and institutions of public order that account for historical and contemporary trends in public disorder. Are there trends toward either expanding or selectively limiting the scope of "disorderly" behavior? Are the police more or less numerous and active now than a century ago? Have judicial and penal policies become consistently more humane and rehabilitative, and more or less effective over time?

By studying the institutions that define and respond to disorder, we begin to deal with the matter of explanation. There are clear historical trends in the magnitude of serious crime in all the cities. There also are evolutionary changes in the character and issues of civil strife. The ultimate theoretical purpose of this kind of study is to understand better the underlying conditions—the socioeconomic and political causes—of these changes. One theoretical approach to crime, promoted especially by critical sociologists like Richard Quinney, is to seek its explanation, hence the origins of changes in its incidence, in the interests of the elites and institutions that selectively define and prosecute it.[1] A parallel argument attributes civil strife to the inequity and repression visited by rulers on the ruled.[2] These political explanations, as we label them, suggest that changes in disorder may be preceded by changes in the composition and interests of elites, especially as observable in changing policies and institutions of public order. To anticipate a conclusion, the hypothesis is only a partial explanation. It accounts for some important changes in the manifestations of civil strife, especially as regards the working class, and also for a number of short-term fluctuations in the official records of crime and punishment. But we find no long-term developments in the policies and institutions of public order that can explain the eruption of mass protest in the last quarter-century or, more important, the long-term trends in common crime. This is in fact one of the principal substantive findings of our study. The similar long-term trends in serious crime to be observed in three of the four cities apparently signify real changes in the social behavior of large numbers of people. And the policies of public order that seem to have "controlled" this behavior in some eras have had no visible effects in others.

Another large class of proposed explanations assumes the objective reality of crime as well as strife, and attributes both phenomena to the socioeconomic rather than the political conditions of society. The socioeconomic sources of disorder include the pressures of population growth and density, patterns of cultural, class, and residential separation, the ebb and flow of economic well-being, and inequities and constrained opportunities in the distribution of money and influence. We find that the inhabitants of the four cities often had good cause to blame some kinds of disorder on such conditions. Comparative study demonstrates that episodes of increased disorder have often followed an increase in some kinds of societal strains, not just in one city but in different times and places. The connection between increasing societal strain and growing disorder is particularly evident in Calcutta. In the three Western cities, by contrast, the evidence is contradictory. The gradual social and economic improvements that paralleled the development of urban public order in the nineteenth century and the first third of the twentieth have continued apace, while at the same time crime and strife increased. Thus on our evidence, either the nature of social causality in Western societies has altered in some fundamental way since World War II, or the celebrated social and economic improvements in urban life in the nineteenth and early twentieth centuries were only indirectly or coincidentally linked to the decline of disorder.

Neither the political nor the socioeconomic approaches to the explanation of public order consistently account for the historical experience of the four cities. The response of officials to burgeoning disorder, though, has seldom been either self-critical or socially reformist. Instead they have designed new mechanisms of control and tinkered with old ones. When disorder is seen to increase, legal and penal codes are revised and police forces are established, expanded, and nationalized; judicial procedures are modified, new penal institutions are established, and alternative strategies of treatment are brought into play. Times of crisis in public order are a stimulus to innovation, and in case after case we can see how officials perceived and responded to episodes of disorder. The next question is whether new policies designed to enhance public order were as efficacious as their advocates hoped or claimed them to be. Even in historical analysis the answers are vexingly tenuous.

General questions about the trends and conditions of public disorder, and the origins and effects of policies of order maintenance, cannot be answered conclusively with information from London, Stockholm, Sydney, and Calcutta. Since three of the cities are Western, the applicability of our generalizations to the cities of the Third World is hypothetical at best. Moreover three of the cities have legal codes and institutions of public order in the English tradition, which simplifies some kinds of comparison but makes it likely that certain observations and conclusions are relatively limited in application. Nonetheless the studies provide sufficient comparative and historical perspective to suggest that most of the prevailing popular, official, and academic explanations of public disorder and how to reduce it are time-bound and culture-bound, which is to say that they are applicable under some conditions and not under others. To make better sense of the subject we need more general theory about the underlying and immediate conditions of public order and disorder. No such theory is proposed here, but the final chapter suggests a general framework for theory, and results of our comparison of the four cities give some substance to it. At the same time the framework reveals the limits even of as broad a comparative study as this one.

It is customary to mention earlier studies that pose the questions or set the procedures of the research at hand. We cannot follow this practice because there has been virtually no comparative historical research on the trends and politics of public order, urban or otherwise. Social scientists have made many comparative studies of civil conflict and some of crime, but few of these works have a historical dimension. The historians interested in public order usually have focused on a single era in a single society. A few scholars, sociologists as well as historians, have traced the changing patterns of disorder and the evolution of policies and institutions of public order over a longer period. For example, we have identified some twenty studies of the changing incidence of crime in Western societies, but only four span a century or more, and only one refers to several societies.

Since the comparative history of public order lacks a distinctive research tradition, we have had to devise one, but we have relied on something other than conventional wisdom in choosing and interpreting the data on which we based our conclusions. Social scientists hold contending conceptions of crime and public order, attach different degrees of significance to data on crime, and have proposed diverse theories about the causes of disorder. The chapter that follows reviews some prevailing conceptual disputes and formulates our views on the meanings and measures of disorder.

NOTES TO PART I, CHAPTER 1

1. See Richard Quinney, *The Social Reality of Crime* (Boston: Little, Brown, 1970) and *Critique of Legal Order* (Boston: Little, Brown, 1973); and also Austin Turk, *Criminality and Legal Order* (Skokie, Ill.: Rand-McNally, 1969).

2. This was Karl Marx's view, of course, and it is characteristic of those who write in the Marxist tradition. Among the contemporary non-Marxist theorists who take a similar theoretical approach to group conflict are Ralf Dahrendorf, *Class and Class Conflict in Industrial Society* (Stanford: Stanford University Press, 1959) and Johan Galtung in various writings.

Chapter 2

CONCEPTIONS AND
MEASURE OF DISORDER

In ordinary English usage "disorder" connotes a threatening lack of predictability in the behavior of others in one's social environment. It refers particularly to the individual and collective acts that are called deviance, crime, and civil strife. There is no point in proposing a universal, denotative definition of social disorder because the objective behaviors so labeled vary from time to time and place to place. In common and historical usage, though, the term is usually associated with actions that threaten the values and interests of the dominant groups in society. Members of such groups wield greatest influence in defining common views of what constitutes "disorder," and theirs are the voices most likely to be heared in historical records.

This study is concerned specifically with *public disorder*, that is, manifestations of social disorder that are the objects of concerted public efforts at control. Public disorder, so defined, has normative, formal, and behavioral facets. In a normative sense, public disorder consists of the threatening activities that large or influential groups think ought to be under public control. The formal boundaries of public disorder are prescribed in legal codes. In practice, public disorder refers to individual and collective actions that are in fact policed and prosecuted. The policies of public order are those which are designed to create and maintain the prevailing conceptions of order; the institutions of public order are the agencies—security and civil police, courts, prisons, training schools—through which policies are implemented.

There is some social disorder in all societies, and it is valid to ask how much and why. But these questions are secondary to our primary interest in understanding the extent to which governments assume responsibility for controlling social disorder and the policies they devise for doing so. In Western societies the processes by which this is accomplished are intrinsically political. Some groups' changing conceptions of order become influential enough to change the legal boundaries of disorderly behavior and, either as a consequence or independently, the practical scope of control activities is adjusted to accommodate the new views. Political leaders and the bureaucracies responsible for maintaining order have a large measure of influence on these processes, but elites and institutions outside government also can act decisively in politicizing social disorder, depending on the times and the nature of the polity. Thus the norms reflected in legal and practical efforts at control are not necessarily as narrow as those of a political elite, nor often as encompassing as the views of the "public" tapped by opinion surveys; rather, they are an amalgam of the norms of various politically influential groups in a society. Since such norms may be diverse and contradictory, their practical consequences for policies of public order share these characteristics. Among the consequences of diversity and change in groups' concerns about disorder are varying and inconsistent patterns of official action.

Both individual and collective actions, "crime" and "civil strife," are included within the ambit of public disorder as it is defined here. It may be asked whether it is useful to study them together, especially since the prevailing empirical tradition is to treat them as distinct phenomena. Behaviorally they are distinct, of course, in the sense that "crime" consists of an aggregate of individual acts, chiefly for individual motives, whereas "civil strife" consists of collective actions entailing some collective objectives. In social and political reality, though, these behaviors often are treated as if they were similar. Both threaten some peoples' sense of well-being, and both lead to concerted demands for the reestablishment of "order." In most contemporary societies the same legal codes define and proscribe crime and various kinds of collective action, and the same or similar institutions of public order are maintained to deal with both conditions.

In a scientific sense we would be justified in juxtaposing crime and civil strife if they tended to occur together, or if there were general theories indicating that they have common antecedents. The evidence on the empirical question of their covariance is fragmentary and inconclusive. The broadest relevant historical study shows that crime and collective violence were generally unrelated in France between 1831 and 1861. In the country as a whole, the incidence of crimes against persons and property varied over time quite independently of the more abrupt variation in collective violence, and comparisons of departments in specific years showed no significant correlations between their levels of crime and collective violence.[1] Contrary evidence comes from a study of much smaller scope, which indicated that in Southern cities in the United States the rise of civil rights demonstrations coincided with a marked short-run decline in violent crimes among blacks.[2] As for theoretical connections between crime and strife, perspectives as diverse as Marxism and structural-functional analysis imply some fundamental similarity in their social origins.[3] We make no a priori assumption about the connections between crime and strife. Both faces of disorder are examined in this study, first because many private citizens and officials respond to them as though they were similar, and second because we think it is worth asking whether and how each has affected the other, and the policies of public order, in the four cities.

CONCEPTIONS OF CRIME

Crime is a complex and culturally relative concept. The activities characterized as crime vary so greatly with respect to perpetrator, purpose, character, and societal response that any search for a valid universal definition of criminal behavior is chimerical. In primitive societies there may be little or no "crime" in the Western sense of formally proscribed behavior that is collectively punished. In the Comanche Indian tribe, for example, behavior contrary to societal norms was ordinarily dealt with through personal means. Homicide committed by someone outside the family required private revenge; wife-stealing was settled by paying off the husband or by revenge against the "thief." Excessive sorcery was the only Comanche "crime" for which the punishment—lynching—was collectivity imposed.[4] Criminal codes—even in more complex societies—vary widely, both among such societies and within them over time. Bloch contended that "there is no such thing as crime in the absolute sense. . . . Definitions as to what is a crime differ greatly from culture to culture and at different times in history. . . ."[5] In ancient Egypt it was criminal to cause the death of a cat; in medieval Europe to dispute the teachings of the Roman Catholic Church; in seventeenth-century England to play at sports on Sunday; and in contemporary South Africa to have sexual relations with someone of another race.

There is a basis for a formal definition of crime that is generally applicable, though. Michael and Adler have argued that "the only possible definition of crime . . . [is] behavior which is prohibited by the criminal code."[6] Such a formal definition is useful for cross-cultural research in that it obviates a search for objectively comparable behaviors and requires instead that we use the standards of the time and place studied. The possibility remains that some of these standards may be universals, or at least so pervasive that they can be treated as constants. Nettler argues, for example, that people have a "timeless desire to be able to move about freely without being robbed or beaten" and that attacks on one's person and property are universally condemned as "wrongs in themselves." Of course all victims of such acts abhor them, and assault and theft seem to be the contemporary criminal activities that figure most prominently in the average person's fear of crime.[7] But "crime" means both more and less than these kinds of acts, socially and legally: "more" because many other kinds of acts are also defined and sanctioned as crime, and "less" because not all attacks on one's person and belongings are labeled and treated as crime.

Murder is a leading candidate for universal condemnation. Contemporary opinion seems to be virtually unanimous that "murder" is a crime and deserves punishment. But that agreement is a function of the use of the label. Some people in every society take others' lives, deliberately or accidentally, directly or indirectly. Unacceptable life taking is ordinarily labeled "murder," and other forms of life taking have different labels—"justifiable use of force," "involuntary manslaughter," and "execution." In Western societies there is something like consensus that deliberate, unprovoked life taking by private individuals is reprehensible, but across societies there are cultural and legal differences regarding what constitutes justifiable provocation.

Much the same argument can be made about "theft," the other candidate for universal crime. Certain ways of acquiring goods are generally rejected and labeled "crime" in contemporary societies; principally these are the private seizure of valuable commodities by force or stealth and without compensation. But the gray area is considerable: businessmen may be able to sell misrepresented or shoddy goods, or charge excessive interest, without penalty. A good many individuals and groups in Western societies subscribe to the notion that other people's property represents ill-gotten gains; thus actions the victims resentfully call "theft" are believed by the takers to be self-righteous retributive or distributive justice. When powerless people seize others' goods their acts are called theft. When politically powerful people seize others' goods, the seizures may be labeled graft, licensing fees, taxation, or nationalization, depending on how they are justified. Our point is not that all such actions should be labeled "theft," but that theft, like murder and all other categories of crime, is an evaluative concept whose precise substantive meaning can be determined only by reference to particular cultures and legal systems.

The cultural relativity of crime is accepted by the substantial majority of contemporary sociologists and criminologists. Virtually none would allege that crime consists of transgressions of the revealed will of God, despite the prevalence of that view in the

Puritanical, Fundamentalist, and Talmudic religious traditions in which a good many Americans, including sociologists and criminologists, have been raised.[8] Some scholars accept, or at least are especially concerned with, Lombrosian theories that crime results from the physiological and mental aberrations of offenders. For most, however, the cultural relativity of crime is a fundamental assumption.[9] It is an assumption of this study also, and one of its implications is that direct comparisons of the levels of criminality across societies are of dubious validity. In fact few such comparisons are made here. Rather, we want to learn how each society's self-defined problems of criminality have changed over time. Such changes, in legal definitions and reports of crime, can be validly compared across societies in ways not applicable to "objective" behavior.

If definitions of crime vary with social and political circumstances, questions about the connection arise. There are two contending academic interpretations of the social origins of criminal law. One is that crime consists of acts that offend strong collective sentiments, that criminal law is the embodiment of moral consensus in a society. Criminal actions occur because individuals have not internalized social norms about proper behavior. In a recent statement of the functional view, Nettler says: "The criminal law . . . *expresses* moral beliefs, it *codifies* them, and it attempts to *enforce* them."[10] In the countervailing view, which is also the newer one, crime consists of acts that offend the perceptions and, especially, threaten the interests of powerful groups in society. Criminal law is the embodiment of the interests of elites, and criminal behavior is a manifestation of nonelite interests. There is an almost dialectical opposition between these two views, which Chambliss has labeled the "functional" and "conflict" theories of crime.[11] Unfortunately most of the research done in these two traditions assumes rather than tests the correctness of the interpretations. From an empirical point of view the accuracy and fruitfulness of the two interpretations surely varies among types of crime and among societies—and indeed they may be equally appropriate. Murder can threaten simultaneously the security of elites and the moral sensibilities of virtually everyone in society. And murder can be perpetrated by individuals who have an objective interest in revenge or gain through murder, although they would be dissuaded from the act if they were adequately socialized in the prevailing norms of society.

This study's assumptions about the nature of crime and criminal law derive from both the functional and conflict traditions. We said earlier that crime is a socially subjective phenomenon. In all societies some men commit assault and homicide, acquire goods by force or fraud, take drugs and alcohol, have extramarital intercourse, slander and disobey their rulers, and otherwise offend their neighbors' sensibilities. Crime is the Western label for acts that violate the norms of society's more influential members so seriously that the acts are legally prohibited and punishments are prescribed for those found guilty. "Deviance" is a somewhat larger and less distinct set of behaviors that violate widely held norms or morality but are not necessarily subject to formal prohibition.

In England, Sweden, and New South Wales, criminal law and prevailing norms appear to have been in approximate agreement about crimes of violence and acquisition, and probably about "serious" crime in general, for most of recent history. The generalization is less applicable to so-called victimless crimes. Influential people in these societies have repeatedly sought to impose standards of conduct on the consumption of alcohol and on gambling, prostitution, and public behavior that runs against the grain of common practice. Generally the moralistic elements have prevailed legally, but the apparent decline in most of the proscribed behaviors probably says more about selective enforcement and practical caution than it does about popular acceptance of legal standards.

In societies having diverse cultural groups, and also in highly stratified societies, conceptions of deviance may differ significantly from one group to another, hence have no close or necessary correspondence to criminality as legally defined. Thus legal definitions typically are a reflection of one group's views about unacceptable behavior. Calcutta can be characterized as such a society throughout most of its history, although more than two distinct groups have been involved and different elites have held power at different times.

In brief, it cannot be assumed a priori that the legal definitions of crime and the control policies used to implement these definitions reflect either social consensus or the interests of an elite. Each assumption presumes an answer to what should be a set of empirical questions about the degree of consensus in any given society on what disorder is, who is threatened by it, and what ought to be done about it. These are among the "political" questions that studies of this kind should address.

CONCEPTIONS OF CIVIL STRIFE

Whereas most crime is viewed with distaste even by the scholars who debate its nature, civil strife is the object of much more ambivalent social and academic attitudes. We mean by the latter overt, collective confrontations between contending groups in a society, including communal and political clashes, economic strikes, antigovernment riots and demonstrations, rebellions, revolutionary movements, and terrorist campaigns. This definition is more inclusive than most others in academic use because it includes nonviolent and nonpolitical strife such as strikes, but it raises few questions of interpretation or objective comparison.[12]

Unlike crime, which exists by reference to prevailing social conceptions and legal definitions, the collective events here labeled civil strife have an objective, behavioral reality: They involve open physical or symbolic combat between groups whose interests conflict. What is problematic about such events is not their reality but the valence of social attitude and political response toward them. Social attitudes toward civil strife depend on whose interests are being advanced or threatened by collective action: One group's "political violence" is another group's "legitimate protest."[13] Rulers' attitudes and response are more uniform, and most such occurrences in the societies we studied are or have been illegal and suppressed whenever they occurred, insofar as governments could suppress them.

The degree of acceptability and the legal status of civil strife nonetheless have changed significantly over time in the four cities, and so have its typical forms and rates of incidence. Strikes and demonstrations are common and widely accepted techniques for promoting group interests in all these societies in the second half of the twentieth century. But in the nineteenth century, when these forms of group action first became common, rulers feared them—sometimes with reason—as fundamental threats to social order, and strenuously attempted to suppress them. The transition from suppression to sufferance and compromise came about more or less rapidly and in quite different circumstances. In Sweden and New South Wales, for example, the urban working classes early and quickly gained political influence within the parliamentary system, and the view of economic strikes as essential and threatening did not long prevail. In Calcutta, by contrast, the strike and the demonstration were widely used in the twentieth century in the service of revolutionary goals, hence were suppressed as long as Bengal remained under colonial rule. That tradition persists in Calcutta, where political strikes and demonstrations are still more intense and ominous events than they are in the other three cities.

A potential for civil strife exists wherever group interests are in conflict, which means virtually everywhere. We make no assumptions about whether the condition is socially desirable or undesirable, though. The citizens and rulers of the four cities evidently have had divergent and changing views on that issue themselves. Thus it is important to determine how popular and official views of strife have changed over time, and under what circumstances. There are certain constants: "Revolutionary" acts of strife will always be anathema to elites and those who identify with them, whereas groups having no effective means to influence those who control their lives are likely to favor collective protest and attack more than those possessing some political power. What does change markedly over time is the extent to which particular kinds of strife become tolerated, and by whom.

THE MEANINGS OF DATA ON DISORDER

Civil strife being quite visible, its occurrence and approximate magnitude are easily detected in societies for which there are numerous official, journalistic, and historical sources. Problems arise mainly with respect to the bias and coverage of the source materials. There is seldom any doubt that reported events did happen, even though their true character may be distorted by the historical records. It also is likely that accounts of most socially consequential events in the four cities have found their way into the records we used.[14]

Unlike custodians of information on illiteracy, employment, hospital beds, tax receipts, and most other social indicators, those responsible for criminal acts seek to conceal data on crime. Admittedly the evidence of homicide is difficult to conceal, and the victims of burglary and robbery generally are aware that the crimes have occurred. Victims of theft do not necessarily report their losses to the police, though, and the much more numerous "victimless" crimes come to official attention only through active police surveillance. The clandestine nature of "crime as legally defined" is compounded by the selective attention given by police to certain kinds of offenders and offenses. Add to this the nonuniform practices of statistical bureaus and courts, and one has ample grounds for agreement with Daniel Bell's assertion that criminal statistics in the United States are about as reliable "as a woman giving her 'correct' age."[15] Presumably there is some correlation between women's self-reports and their true ages, which implies that self-reports (and crime statistics) can be used as indicators rather than precise measures of what they purport to be about. Austin Turk is representative of scholars who reject even this possibility. He dismisses "official crime statistics and data obtained from and about persons identified publicly as criminals" as "simply not directly relevant" for identifying and studying patterns of criminal behavior.[16]

Despite the extreme skepticism of some critics, the conventional approach to official crime statistics is to acknowledge the manifold sources of "error" in the processes by which they are generated, then to treat them as approximate indicators of objective criminal behavior. This is not entirely an act of faith. Various unofficial studies have been made of crimes of violence and acquisition, mostly in the United States but also in Britain. They include observation of delinquents, self-reports of criminal activity, and opinion surveys of victimization. When the results are compared with official statistics, it is evident that the latter substantially understate the total volume of criminal behavior by ratios from 2:1 to 10:1. But the comparisons also show that the *relative* frequency of crimes mentioned in victimization surveys corresponds closely to the *relative* frequency of crimes known to the police. Moreover, as Nettler concludes in a summary of such studies, "the social conditions associated with high rates of serious crimes known to the police are also, with some qualifications, associated with high rates of victimization."[17] In other words, the various sources of official and unofficial information on crimes of violence and acquisition all seem to reflect the same underlying behavioral realities.

According to Thorsten Sellin, the "best" kinds of official indicators are those which are closest to the source of crime from the standpoint of administrative procedure, that is, those based on reports of "crime known to police." Reported crimes will be fewer in number than the total of all criminal acts, but more numerous than arrests, and still more numerous than cases brought to trial and cases resulting in conviction. Data on some kinds of crime also are said to be much more accurate than data on others: Reports of homicides are thought to be more precise than reports of crime against property, and data on both are more accurate than reports of "victimless" crimes. More recent data are generally claimed to be more accurate than historical data because of standardization of reporting procedures. Data from some countries are said to be a good deal more reliable than data from others, given irregularities and inconsistencies in the processes by which crime information is categorized and summarized.[18] The principal authority on crime data in the United States has said that the country has collected "the worst crime statistics of any major country in the Western world,"[19] but Swedish consultants to this study claim that Swedish data on the subject are quite accurate.

Much of the debate over the "accuracy" of crime statistics results from attempts to assess the "true" extent of criminal behavior. Perhaps that is the wrong avenue to explore; certainly it seems to be the wrong issue to try to settle with official crime statistics. In this study we are concerned with two equally important questions, which are more readily answered with the data available. First, we are concerned with the extent of crime *as a social and political reality*. Hence we are especially interested in how much popular and official concern there is about crime, and how much public effort is directed at it. Table I.2.1 summarizes information on the availability, reliability, and meanings of data on criminality in Western societies. The column specifying the significance of the measures reveals that public and especially official concern are precisely the kinds of conditions most directly represented by the more widely available indicators of

Table I.2.1 Data and Indicators of Criminality in Western Societies

Data	Source	Availability of comparative data[a]	Prima facie significance of indicators[b]	Validity of information[c]
Criminal behavior	Self-reports	Scattered questionnaire studies, mostly in the U.S. after 1960, mostly of juveniles	Extent of individual criminal behavior	Honesty of respondents is doubtful, but self-reports show crime rates much higher than police records
Victimization	Surveys of victims	A few sample surveys, mostly in U.S. cities, after 1960	Impact of crime on ordinary citizens	Presumably good for victims of assault and theft; imply "true" crime rates two to ten times greater than police records
Crimes known to police	Police records	Reported for serious crimes in many Western societies beginning in mid- to late nineteenth century, for minor offenses somewhat later	Extent of citizen and police concern with crime	For crimes with victims, markedly influenced by citizen trust in police; for crimes without victims, a function of police surveillance; for both a function of recording systems
Arrests	Police records	Similar to above, "Crimes known to police"	Extent of police action against suspected criminals	Generally good but affected by recording and reported practices
Committals to trial	Higher court records	Serious crimes only, usually reported or knowable pre-1800[d]	Extent of official concern with serious crime	Good except where cases are shifted among jurisdictions or between higher and lower courts

Table I.2.1 (continued)

Court convictions	Higher court records	Same as above, "committals to trial"d	Extent of official sanctions against serious crime	Good
Cases disposed of summarily	Lower court records	Minor crimes only; not reported consistently until late nineteenth or early twentieth centuries	Extent of official sanctions against minor crime	Variable, affected by recording and reporting practices
Executions	Administrative records	Same as "Court convictions," above	Severity of official sanctions against crime	Excellent
Prison population	Administrative records	National and some local jurisdictions from late nineteenth century, some earlier data	Impact of sanctions on convicted criminals	Good in twentieth century, incomparable during much of 1800s because of extensive use of workhouses, transportation, etc.

a. These judgments are based on first-hand knowledge of the countries and cities studied, and selective reading of the literature, but they gloss over great differences among countries. In England and Wales the first national crime statistics, on committals to trial for serious offenses, were compiled beginning in 1805; detailed and comprehensive data are available after 1856. In the United States, which has lagged far behind most other Western nations in this regard, national compilation of "uniform" crime statistics dates only from 1933. Before that, data are available only for some states and cities, though certain of these series extend back into the eighteenth century.

b. This column suggests the simplest and most direct interpretation of indicators constructed from the comparative data. By "indicators" we mean aggregated data expressed as a ratio to population (e.g., "murders per 100,000").

c. "Validity" refers to the accuracy with which the indicators are likely to measure the conditions listed under "Prima facie significance."

d. The activities of higher courts before the introduction of national reporting systems can be determined by analysis of court records and reports. This laborious process has been carried out only in a few countries and jurisdictions.

crime. This is not a novel insight. Bloch used American data on delinquency to demonstrate that they index public and official attitudes at least as much as delinquent behavior,[20] and much of the critical and revisionist literature in criminology suggests that crime statistics reflect the interests of the public order system. It is remarkable that there have been so few attempts to act on that insight by analyzing what crime data signify about the concerns, norms, and practices of those who define and maintain public order.[21]

This does not imply that the "true" volume of criminal behavior can be ignored. Here we part company with the revisionist critics. Surely it is important to determine whether the nature and extent of real criminal behavior (as legally defined) affect the extent of public and official concern about crime. It is equally important to know whether policies designed to control disorder affect actual behavior, or only the sense of concern. The self-reporting and victimization surveys mentioned previously provide rather direct ways of ascertaining the extent of objective criminal behavior, but they are too new and few to permit us to say with certainty whether changes in behavior are accompanied by changes in public concern and official statistics. Thus despite the desirability of having direct information about the extent of criminal behavior, we must do without such data for the cities and eras studied here. Under some circumstances, though, it may be possible to draw valid inferences, not about the actual volume of criminal behavior, but about how it changes over time.

The second question of particular interest involves how problems of public order change over time. Given our argument about the social and political reality of crime, statistics on reported crime and arrests in most contemporary societies are, in effect, the reports of the social and political system to itself about the seriousness of self-defined problems of public order. As public concern mounts, more crimes are likely to be reported; and as police concern rises, so will patrolling and arrests. Similarly, changes in the extent of official insecurity are likely to show up in changing rates of committals for trial, convictions, and—depending on the time and place—the severity of sentences. Evidently there is a circular process in which increasing concern is likely to generate higher rates of reported crime, and the reports themselves substantially influence judgments about whether policies of public order are working or in need of revision, whether officials and public institutions are competent or incompetent, and ultimately whether society at large is "healthy" or "sick."[22] Crime statistics are thus both consequence and cause of public and official concern. This may be an intensely frustrating problem for those who want to know what changing crime rates "really" mean; but for our purposes changes in crime statistics—especially large changes—become a telling indicator of changes in the magnitude of public order problems and of changes in policies for dealing with them.

We have made the point that the relation between the true extent of crime and public concern about crime is unknowable in most present and all past circumstances. But that does not mean that changes in the two are unrelated. It is plausible, in fact, that within any given society an approximate interrelation exists between changes in public concern and in criminal behavior. As particularly threatening behavior increases in frequency, for example, concern and official reaction are likely to increase, perhaps slowly at first, then more rapidly than the behavior itself. Concern about crime can grow independently of behavioral change, of course, but when this happens increased official action will probably follow, having the effect of "creating" more criminal behavior by legal definition and labeling. The basic point is still valid: The extent of criminal behavior is likely to vary over time in approximate relation to public and official concern about criminality. Therefore the *trends* in crime statistics are revealing about criminal behavior in ways that statistics for one point in time cannot be. Since changes in concern and behavior exert mutual effects only gradually, the interpretation of year-to-year changes in crime statistics is problematic. Trends of five to ten years' duration and longer are much more significant. Directly they tell of changes in public and official concern; indirectly they may permit inferences about the direction of change in criminal behavior.

These interpretations of crime statistics assume that the data are generated by police and courts which are mainly concerned with controlling criminal behavior. The assumption is warranted for the three Western cities in the study; it is not valid for Calcutta in the twentieth century. During the last 40 years of British rule in Bengal, and during the decades since independence in 1947, Calcutta was swept by recurring episodes of intense political, economic, and communal strife that posed far graver threats to public order than ordinary crime. Under these pressures the police and courts gave less and less attention to crime and in several periods seem to have virtually ceased operations. The fluctuations of reported crime in Calcutta in the twentieth century reveal much about official concern with crime, but not in the usual way: The rulers were distracted by larger crises that threatened their very survival. Calcutta illustrates a general point: Crime statistics generated by effective institutions under "normal" social conditions mean one thing, statistics generated by decaying institutions under conditions of crisis usually mean something quite different.

CATEGORIES AND INDICATORS OF DISORDER

Whatever conceptual meaning is imputed to official data on crime and punishment, any effort to compare and contrast the data across time and among cities encounters a host of technical problems. One set of problems concerns categorization of different kinds of criminal behavior: Should it be done at all, and if so, how? A more fundamental matter is the comprehensiveness and reliability of the data available for the four cities. Whatever data are available can be compared over time only when weighted by population, which poses fresh problems related to the availability and accuracy of demographic data. Brief diagnoses of these problems follow, and our approaches to each are sketched.

Categories of Crime

Different kinds of criminal behavior inspire different degrees of concern and are differentially policed and reported; therefore they must be compared separately. The criminal codes of the four societies furnish one possible point of departure. They are in substantial agreement in their formal definitions of criminal behavior, which reflect the common cultural heritage of the three Western cities and the historical and political circumstance that Australian and Indian criminal codes descend from English common law. There are indigenous accretions and adaptations, especially in Indian law, but its basic framework remains English. There are two prohibitive barriers to employing the official categories for comparisons as given. One is their sheer number and detail. In the 1890s crime in London was reported and prosecuted under 149 specific categories organized under seven more general headings, and the criminal code of New South Wales was equally detailed. There is little if any reason to compare the relative incidence of most of the specific categories. The fine Anglo-Australian distinction between "rogue" and "notorious rogue," for example, surely makes or made no difference except to the handful of unfortunate scoundrels relegated to the latter category. And it is of some intrinsic but no comparative interest that nineteenth century New South Welshmen could be prosecuted if found "wandering with Aborigines," or that the crime returns from the London Metropolitan Police District in the early years of Queen Victoria's reign list the unique offense of "presenting a pistol at Her Majesty the Queen with intent to alarm her."

Similar and overlapping categories can always be combined for analytic purposes. The more serious problem is that categories have been repeatedly and inconsistently combined, divided, and recombined for administrative convenience in each city. New categories of offenses are defined, and old ones lapse into desuetude or are subsumed by other categories. Some categories are shuffled from one general heading to another, while the headings themselves undergo subtle and sometimes dramatic changes of scope. Generally the categories according to which crime is reported and prosecuted vary more widely within each city than among them. This tendency can be most instructive about the evolving interests and concerns of the officials who create the data, but it raises hob with systematic study of trends.[23]

Our approach has been to distinguish four general types of offenses that subsume most of the more detailed categories used in crime reports. In a few analyses all types of crime within each general category are aggregated; usually, though, comparisons are made using more specific subcategories within each. The general categories are as follows.

1. Crimes of aggression, including murder and attempts, woundings, and assault. Where official statistics permit, and they usually do, the offenses of rape, abortion, and assault in the course of robbery are excluded from this general category.

2. Crimes of acquisition, including all illegal means of acquiring money and property. White-collar crimes such as fraud and embezzlement are analyzed separately from common theft. Three different forms of theft also are distinguished in the criminal codes of the societies studied here, and in some of our analyses. In increasing order of seriousness, they are larceny, burglary, and robbery. A number of less common property offenses such as counterfeiting and receiving stolen goods are included in aggregate measures of crimes of acquisition.

3. Crimes against morality and custom include both sexual offenses and various "victimless crimes."[24] The offenses of sexual assault, deviance, and prostitution are treated as one subset of these crimes, drunkenness as another. Also under this heading we put vagrancy, gambling, and other behaviors thought to be disorderly, nonproductive, or otherwise offensive to prevailing standards of public conduct. Since the latter activities are so diverse, they are considered separately, if at all, rather than in the aggregate.

4. Crimes against public order include such instances of overt resistance to authorities as rioting, assaults on police and other officials, and prohibited political activities. Serious political offenses of this kind are rare in all the cities. In some of the cities violations of administrative regulations also are analyzed separately from offenses that are specifically political.

Several points need to be made about these general categories. First, they are not absolutely distinct, either in concept or application. Drunks resisting arrest may be found guilty of attacking police (category 4) or merely disorderly conduct (category 3), depending on the mores and procedures of the day and place. On the other hand it can be assumed that the first two general categories, crimes of aggression and acquisition, refer to quite similar kinds of objectively defined behavior in all four cities.[25] Second, some of our analyses distinguish between more and less serious offenses of each general category. Offenses that are dealt with by higher courts were and are "serious" by prevailing official definition, but those dealt with summarily can usually be assumed to be "minor." There is no particular consistency within or among cities about which offenses are treated in which way, and specific cases may be processed one way or the other depending on circumstance. We employ no "objective" definition of serious crime; rather, the measures of serious crime reflect prevailing official views about which kinds of offenses, and which offenders, are important enough to require the full and expensive attention of prosecutors, courts, and juries.[26]

Availability of Data

Before this study could begin, it was necessary to be sure that sufficient usable data on disorder could be found for the cities. Some general observations are summarized in Table I.2.1; more specific information is given in Table I.2.2. Data available for the early nineteenth century refer only or mainly to criminal cases committed to trial in the highest courts. Thus they provide an index to concern among the elites about "serious" crime, but no direct information about the extent of public concern with crime or the overall volume of official efforts to maintain order. Information on crimes known to the police and arrests begins to be reported later in the century, usually in summary fashion at first, then with increasing detail. Cases tried summarily—by magistrates, police courts, or their equivalents— were first reported at about the same time as arrests. These different kinds of data are subject to somewhat different interpretations, as suggested in Table I.2.1. When most or all data are available for the same period, as they are for more than a century in some instances, their variations can be compared over time. This kind of comparison gives information about the complex interactions among criminal behavior, public concern, and official action that could never be inferred from the analysis of the measures separately.

Most information on civil strife is found in narrative form and is not readily reduced to quantitative indicators. One exception is information on strikes, including number of incidents, participants, and working days lost. Official data on the subject have been compiled annually in the twentieth century for all Britain, though not for London separately, and for New South Wales. In our research more or less consistent information on strikes was compiled from various

Table I.2.2 The Availability of Principal Data Series on Crime and
Strikes in the Four Cities[a]

Type of data	London[b]	Stockholm	Sydney[c]	Calcutta[d]
Crimes reported or known to police	1858-1974	1841-1971	1952-1970	1800-1971
Arrests	1857-1931, 1947-1974	—	1879-1893, 1914-1970	1871-1958
Accused/committed to trial	1820-1974	1841-1947	1811-1824, 1859-1971	1871-1971
Convictions for indictable crimes or higher court cases	1820-1974	1830-1951	1811-1971	1871-1971
Convictions for lesser offenses or cases disposed of summarily	1857-1913 1949-1974	1841-1951	1879-1893, 1914-1970	1920-1958
Strikes	1893-1974	1901-1970	1912-1970	1920-1958

a. These are the maximum periods for which data could be obtained for this study. Data are missing for some years in some series. Few series are precisely comparable over time because of changes in jurisdiction and procedure, scope and detail of coverage, and definition of categories of offenses.

b. Crime data are for the County of Middlesex (including the City of London), 1820-1873; and for the Metropolitan Police District (excluding the City of London) ca. 1857-1974. Strike data are for all Britain. After 1931 the statistics on higher court activities are total cases only. Data on summary drunkenness and prostitution offenses are available for longer periods than other classes of data.

c. Data for New South Wales. Statistics on convictions for lesser offenses were not used in this study.

d. Data before 1870 include fragmentary statistics for all Bengal from East India Company reports from 1800 to 1840 and data for Calcutta for eighteen years between 1840 and 1870. Data for the early 1940s are missing.

sources, mainly official ones, for Stockholm and Calcutta.

Cities have long been the seats of higher courts as well as a principal source of the courts' business, and the first modern police forces were established in response to distinctly urban problems of order. Thus one consideration that influenced our initial focus on cities, rather than on regions or entire nations, was the expectation that they would provide earlier and more reliable information on crime and public order.[27] This expectation was borne out. Quite unexpectedly, however, crime data for Calcutta, London, and Stockholm in recent decades are sparser than they were half a century ago. For Calcutta the detailed reports appear not to have been published after the late 1950s, and only summary data are published in national sources—the most useful, *Crime in India,* being restricted to official use. In London, fiscal constraints imposed by the Depression and the policies of a new commissioner of police, led to the sharp curtailment of public reporting of criminal and judicial statistics after 1931. More complete data were published beginning in 1947, but the reporting of data on trials and convictions for various offense categories has never been resumed. Such statistics are reported at the county and national level, but the Metropolitan Police District data are thereby comingled with those of several counties. Something similar happens to crime data on Stockholm beginning in the 1950s: After this time the data are less detailed than previously, and statistics on convictions have not been reported since the early 1960s. One partial explanation is that officials in both Sweden and Britain are more concerned with recording and dealing with crime on a nationwide basis than on an urban scale.[28]

Cities and Other Jurisdictions

A deceptively difficult problem in this kind of study is matching crime and population data. Since we want to identify and diagnose changes in the relative incidence of reported crime, the raw data in official reports must be weighted by population.[29] The available data on population and crime do not always refer to the same social entity, however, and we often have had to settle for measures that refer to something other than "the city" as conventionally defined.[30] The subjects we portray statistically have been defined for us by the scope of the available data—that is, data from jurisdictions that do not necessarily or consistently coincide with the administrative or demographic boundaries of urban areas. Each city poses a somewhat different set of matching problems.

London: London has had no single administrative boundary for most of its history. Our data for crime and population prior to 1869 refer to the County of Middlesex, which at the beginning of the century included substantial rural and suburban areas but excluded the urban concentration south of the Thames. By the 1830s the demographic city had spread well beyond the boundaries of Middlesex, and the new Metropolitan Police District (MPD) reflected one administrative conception of the city's boundaries. After 1869 the data used here refer to the MPD, which has continued to expand more or less in concert with urban sprawl. The MPD notably excludes the City of London (the financial district), which historically has been separately policed, or unpoliced. The City has had a small and shrinking population during the last century, never more than two percent of the people living in the MPD.

Stockholm: The data on crime and population in Stockholm refer throughout the nineteenth and twentieth centuries to the city as administratively defined; but the administrative boundaries have changed over time and have consistently excluded many suburbs (until 1971, when the first steps were taken toward an integrated administration of the City and County of Stockholm). In 1968, for example, administrative Stockholm included only 59 percent of the population of Greater Stockholm as statistically defined; the remaining 41 percent were outside the scope of the data on crime that.we use here.

Calcutta: The estimates of Calcutta's population are not particularly reliable at any time. That uncertainty compounds another imprecision: For much of the nineteenth century the crime reports referred mainly to the town of Calcutta, but the population estimates included suburbs. Moreover the judicial statistics apparently included cases from elsewhere in Bengal. Viewed in light of the limited and selective scope of Western institutions of public order in Calcutta, though, these problems fade in significance. We mentioned earlier, moreover, that in the twentieth century the exigencies of civil conflict have recurrently preoccupied the police. Crime data for Calcutta thus are mainly a function of the scope of police activities within some rather small but not constant segment of the city's enormous, sprawling population. Far from helping to quantify criminal behavior, they may not even be a good indicator of official concern—because other matters weigh so heavily that crime is of relatively little moment.[31]

Sydney: Sydney was founded in 1788, and its population is known with reasonable accuracy from that date; but the police and judicial statistics for the city as administratively defined proved far too scant for our purposes. Our solution has been to use data on crime and population for New South Wales in its entirety. Sydney is and always has been the metropole and administrative capital of the colony, later state, as well as the hub of its commercial and cultural activity; thus it is reasonable to assume that patterns of crime in New South Wales are those of Sydney writ large. Still, in demographic terms the population of metropolitan Sydney has comprised as little as 25 percent of the state's population (in the 1850s) and as much as 60 percent (in 1970).

This chapter has reviewed some implications of different conceptions of crime and strife for the comparative study of public disorder. We also have reported our views about the prospects and pitfalls of constructing comparative measures of crime, and the interpretations which can and cannot be put on them. Readers may not agree with our interpretations and solutions, but at least they know what principles guided our research and analyses.

NOTES TO PART I, CHAPTER 2

1. Abdul Q. Lodhi and Charles Tilly, "Urbanization, Crime, and Collective Violence in 19th Century France," *American Journal of Sociology*, 79 (September 1973), 296-318. The study does not examine the more plausible possibility that crime and collective violence are correlated over time within particular cities or departments, perhaps for want of sufficient data.

2. F. Solomon et al., "Civil Rights Activity and Reduction in Crime Among Negroes," *Archives of General Psychiatry*, 12 (March 1965), 227-236.

3. William J. Chambliss, *Functional and Conflict Theories of Crime* (New York: MSS Modular Publications, 1974, Module 17), derives a Marxist theory of crime from the same premises used by Marxists to account for group conflict. Two major functionalist statements about the origins of crime and collective behavior are, respectively, Emile Durkheim, "Crime as Normal Behavior," in David Dressler, ed., *Readings in Criminology and Penology* (New York: Columbia University Press, 1972), an extract from Durkheim's *The Division of Labor in Society* (New York: Free Press, 1949); and Talcott Parsons, "Certain Primary Sources and Patterns of Aggression in the Social Structure of the Western World," in Lyman Bryson et al., eds., *Conflicts of Power in Modern Culture* (New York: Conference on Science, Philosophy, and Religion, Seventh Symposium, 1947).

4. The example is cited by E. Adamson Hoebel, "Plains Indian Law in Development: The Comanche," in Donald Cressey and David Ward, eds., *Delinquency, Crime and Social Process* (New York: Harper & Row, 1969).

5. Herbert Bloch, *Disorganization: Personal and Social* (New York: Knopf, 1952), p. 258.

6. Jerome Michael and Mortimer Adler, *Crime, Law and Social Science* (New York: Harcourt, 1933), p. 2.

7. Gwynn Nettler, *Explaining Crime* (New York: McGraw-Hill, 1974), pp. 2-5.

8. On the religious foundations of law among the Puritans and Hebrews see, respectively, George Haskins, *Law and Authority in Early Massachusetts* (New York: Macmillan, 1960) and Hyman Goldin, *Hebrew Criminal Law and Procedure* (New York: Twayne, 1952).

9. The most influential exponent of biological theories of criminality was Cesare Lombroso (1835-1909); see his *Crime: Its Causes and Remedies* (Boston: Little, Brown, 1911). His original argument that criminals are throwbacks to our primitive ancestors is still influential in Mediterranean and Latin American criminology. One contemporary manifestation of the biological approach in North America and northern Europe is the search for genetic "flaws" in

perpetrators of crimes of violence. For reviews of the biological approach, in its historical and contemporary manifestations, see Hermann Mannheim, *Comparative Criminology* (Boston: Houghton Mifflin, 1965), chs. 12 and 13, and Donald Mulvilhill and Melvin Tumin, *Crimes of Violence, Report to the National Commission on the Causes and Prevention of Violence*, vol. 12 (Washington, D.C.: Government Printing Office, 1969), ch. 7. The biological and cultural approaches are not mutually exclusive because factors of both kinds may influence criminal behavior. Our view is that the cultural and situational factors so modify the biological factors that the latter have little independent explanatory power.

10. Nettler, op. cit., p. 36. She adds the obvious qualification that the relation between criminal law and a people's moral beliefs is imprecise and changes over time.

11. This characterization of functional and conflict theories is drawn from Chambliss, op. cit.

12. There are well-established research traditions in political science and sociology for the collection and comparison of data on collective actions that are variously labeled "collective" or "political" violence, "conflict" or "instability" events. The terms are not used pejoratively but to denote sets of empirically similar occurrences. For a brief survey of this research through 1971 see T. R. Gurr, "The Calculus of Civil Conflict," *Journal of Social Issues*, 28 (No. 1, 1972). There is a parallel tradition for the comparative study of strikes; see, for example, Arthur M. Ross and George W. Hartmann, *Changing Patterns of Industrial Conflict* (New York: Wiley, 1960), and Douglas A. Hibbs, Jr., *Industrial Conflict in Advanced Industrial Societies* (Cambridge: Center for International Studies, MIT, 1974). The term "civil strife" here refers to all such occurrences, whereas elsewhere the first author has used it to refer to a somewhat less inclusive set of events; see "A Comparative Study of Civil Strife," in Hugh Davis Graham and T. R. Gurr, eds., *Violence in America: Historical and Comparative Perspectives, A Report to the National Commission on the Causes and Prevention of Violence* (New York: Praeger and Bantam Books, 1969), ch. 17.

13. There is heated academic and social debate about the labeling of such phenomena and especially about the theoretical uses and normative implications of the term "political violence." Two of the less muddled commentaries on the controversy are Terry Nardin, *Violence and the State: A Critique of Empirical Political Theory* (Beverly Hills, Calif.: Sage Professional Papers in Comparative Politics, no. 020, 1971), and Kenneth W. Grundy and Michael A. Weinstein, *The Ideologies of Violence* (Columbus: Merrill, 1974). The more neutral and comprehensive term "civil strife" is used in this study to avoid the appearance of normative judgment.

14. Contemporary studies of civil strife have revealed that the number and types of events identified vary markedly according to the journalistic source used; see Charles R. Doran et al., "A Test of Cross-National Event Reliability: Global Versus Regional Data Sources," *International Studies Quarterly*, 17 (June 1973), 175-204. The four city studies rely on a variety of historical sources, but they cannot be assumed to be absolutely comprehensive. We found virtually no references to civil strife in Calcutta during the nineteenth century, for example,

and this seems somewhat unlikely in view of its turbulent twentieth century history. Nineteenth century Stockholm, according to standard histories, was also a relatively peaceful city except for a few politically consequential riots and demonstrations. Archival research by Leif Persson and Sven Sperlings for this study, however, produced evidence of many small-scale riots and brawls between citizens and police or soldiers.

15. Daniel Bell, "The Myth of Crime Waves," in *The End of Ideology* (New York: Free Press, 1960), p. 157, cited in Herbert A. Bloch and Gilbert Geis, *Man, Crime, and Society: The Forms of Criminal Behavior* (New York: Random House, 1962), p. 164.

16. Turk, op. cit., p. 8.

17. Nettler, op. cit., ch. 4, quotation from p. 72.

18. See Bloch and Geis' useful review of evidence on "The Extent of Crime," Part 3 in *Man, Crime, and Society*. Other general discussions include Fred P. Graham, "A Contemporary History of American Crime," in Graham and Gurr, eds., *Violence in America*, ch. 13; and ch. 2, "American Criminal Statistics: An Explanation and Appraisal," in Mulvilhill and Tumin, *Crimes of Violence*, vol. 11. All these appraisals are concerned almost exclusively with crime data from North America. A general commentary on the sources, uses, and limitations of criminal statistics with special reference to Britain, is Mannheim, *Comparative Criminology*, chp. 5. The accuracy of British historical statistics on the subject has been heatedly debated. J. J. Tobias, *Crime and Industrial Society in the Nineteenth Century* (London: Batsford, 1967), categorically dismisses most nineteenth century English crime statistics. V. A. C. Gatrell and T. B. Hadden, who have made much more systematic use of those data than Tobias, conclude that they are very informative, especially about characteristics of offenders and trends in crime, in "Criminal Statistics and Their Interpretation," E. A. Wrigley, ed., *Nineteenth Century Society* (Cambridge: The University Press, 1972), pp. 336-396. The adequacy of contemporary Australian data on crime is discussed in Paul Wilson and J. Brown, *Crime and the Community* (St. Lucia: University of Queensland Press, 1973).

19. Thorsten Sellin, quoted by Fred P. Graham, "A Contemporary History."

20. Herbert A. Bloch, "Juvenile Delinquency: Myth or Threat?" *Journal of Criminal Law*, 49 (November-December, 1958), 303-309.

21. One of a class of exceptions is Turk's analysis of United States crime data with reference to what they imply about differences between the norms enforced by officials and the norms of various population groups, in ch. 5 of *Criminality and Legal Order*.

22. An important qualification is that public and elite concern about crime often increases in response, not to crime rates per se, but to the widely publicized occurrence of a few particularly dramatic acts. Our research on Sydney offered a number of examples. Moreover the importance of crime statistics evidently varies among societies. Where there are autocratic elites and repressive institutions, such data serve mainly a self-monitoring function for officials responsible for maintaining order and, as in the Soviet Union, they may never be made public. In more open societies they have more widespread impact, public and private.

23. An example is provided by the difficulties of tracing the changing incidence of murder in Stockholm over an extended period. From 1841 to 1886 reported murders are aggregated in official reports with manslaughter and attempted murder. Between 1886 and 1909 the problem is compounded by the inclusion of infanticide. After 1910 the reports distinguish among all three kinds

of offenses plus a fourth, procuring abortion. The judicial statistics on convictions, however, are aggregated quite differently. Convictions for attempted murder, murder, and manslaughter combined are reported from 1830 through 1909; convictions for infanticide and procuring abortion are separately reported until 1878, then in combination until 1912. After 1912, however, convictions for all four offenses are reported in a summary annual figure, without breakdowns. The sources are various administrative and statistical reports of the city government.

24. The concept of victimless crime makes some social sense when restricted to illegal sexual acts between consenting adults and to the use of mild narcotics and stimulants. But it is appallingly callous to apply this characterization to alcoholism, drug addiction, chronic gambling, and prostitution. The personal and social costs for most of the individuals involved are high indeed. A pressing social issue in Western societies is whether such people ought to be treated as criminals or as victims in need of help.

25. This is not to say that the magnitudes of such behaviors can therefore be compared directly, only that the offenses as legally defined and reported are similar.

26. For much of the nineteenth century there are data only on serious offenses (i.e., on those processed by the higher courts). Therefore comparisons of crime data over the very long run usually must be limited to "serious" offenses.

27. Almost all the historical studies of the subject in the United States have had an urban focus.

28. The official sources of data on crime and punishment are cited in the city studies.

29. Few of the official sources used in these studies report rates of crime (i.e., numbers of offenses per 10,000 or 100,000 population). All rates used are our calculation, which raises questions about the reliability of population estimates. At least such estimates are better than the raw data on crime because they are more easily determined, hence more accurate, and because there are no obvious reasons for error in them to be systematic (i.e., consistently higher or lower than the correct figures).

Throughout this study we follow the conventional practice of calculating rates by weighting crime data by total population, even though rates of reported crime vary widely among sex, age, and class groups. Sometimes data on the demographic characteristics of offenders are known. But such data are reported too rarely and inconsistently for us to use them for systematic comparisons over time.

30. Conventional definitions of cities refer to the concentration and spatial distribution of population. In the academic literature they are widely modified by reference to such variables as lifeways and patterns of interaction. Charles Tilly offers a good review of different approaches to the definition of communities and cities in An Urban World (Boston: Little, Brown, 1974), pp. 18-31.

31. Similar interpretations might conceivably be made of crime data from the other cities, especially in the nineteenth century. The difference is that in Calcutta no other interpretation is plausible.

PART II

THE COMPARATIVE ANALYSIS
OF PUBLIC ORDER

CHAPTER 1

THE BEST OF TIMES, THE WORST OF TIMES:
Trends in Crime in Four Societies

The four cities have had different experiences of crime and strife during the past century and a half. In London, Stockholm, and New South Wales the official indicators of common crimes of violence and theft all trace a declining trend during the second half of the nineteenth century and into the early decades of the twentieth century. But no later than the 1950s, most of them begin a dramatic ascent. One might almost conclude that some common social and political dynamics created public order over the course of a century in Western societies, then went crazily unsprung in a single generation. When we examine the regulation of social conduct, though, evidence of common trends in behavior is overshadowed by many indications that the tides of official concern with deviant and disorderly behavior have periodically risen and subsided. Civil conflict in the Western cities also has been episodic. A recurrent issue of conflict has been the demands of rising classes for a greater share of goods and power; but open combat over these and other issues has erupted at different times, displaying differing forms and intensities, and bringing varied consequences. Calcutta represents another world with a vastly different history. Its orderly colonial existence at the turn of the twentieth century disintegrated in a welter of crime, conflict, and repression in the first half of the present century. The "creative" uses of disorder that won Indian independence endured in Calcutta long after their initial goal was achieved. Reported crime, prosecutions, and convictions oscillated wildly in the first 25 years after independence, in a complex response to the ebb and flow of political combat.

The evidence for these generalizations, and many qualifications of them, are the subject of this chapter and the next. We begin by examining the trends in official indicators of crime, and we also deal with the critical question of interpretation: Are the trends a reflection of changing social behavior or changing institutional policies? The next chapter surveys the comparative history of civil conflict in the four cities, with special reference to its national political context, and identifies the principal periods of crisis in public order in each of the societies.

The grist for the analysis that follows is provided by indicators constructed from offical data on several categories of crime, using both offenses known to police and convictions, whenever both are available. Interpretation is problematic, however for reasons spelled out previously. Depending on their types, indicators of crime are directly informative about the volume of citizens' reports to police, the extent of police activity, and the extent and severity of public sanctions applied. But virtually no one who studies crime statistics is content to stop there. Where there's smoke there's fire, they assume, and differences in the volume of smoke should tell us where the fire is greatest. We think the assumption is tenable under certain strict conditions. Differences in crime indicators from one locale to another permit inferences about differences in social behavior only if the locales have very similar policing agencies, operating with similar legal codes, procedures, and methods of accounting. The greater the differences in any of these institutional factors, the less reliable are inferences about differential social behavior. In this study these conditions for comparability do not obtain. As a result, few conclusions can be drawn about differences among the cities in absolute levels of crime.

Differences in crime indicators within one locale over time are more promising, provided the offense in question is a "visible" one. Crimes that have victims usually are more consistently recorded than those whose detection depends on active policing: People who are assaulted or plundered complain; gamblers, addicts, sexual deviants, drunks, and abortionists generally keep a low profile. Therefore the trends in common crimes against persons and property offer potential evidence about changes in social behavior. Additional evidence is found by reference to different indicators of the same kind of offense: If change is similar in indicators of both reported crime and convictions, or indicators of similar kinds of offenses (both murder and assault, or robbery and larceny), we gain confidence about the social reality of change. Another test is whether substantial changes have occurred in the institutions and practices of policing and judicial administration, and if so, whether they may account for recorded changes in crime. Small or abrupt changes in the indicators are suspect on these grounds. Changes that are both large and cumulative are more convincing evidence of behavioral change.

Our analysis focuses on long-term trends in representative indicators of murder and assault, theft, white-collar crime, sexual deviance, and drunkenness. The primary concern is to describe the trends, the secondary is to interpret them in the light of what we know about changing policies of public order. The question of interpretation is only begun here; the analysis of legal and institutional innovation in later chapters yields additional evidence.

A preliminary note on methods is needed. The graphic comparisons below are based, wherever possible, on ten-year moving averages of annual crime data, weighted per 100,000 population. All subsequent references to crime "rates" and "indicators" are to these population-weighted measures. They convey no direct evidence on the absolute number of offenses or on year-to-year variations. Since our objective is to include the longest time span possible for each type of offense for each city, it is generally necessary to use several different kinds of measures on a single chart. Where possible, we use two parallel kinds of indicators, one based on offenses known (or arrests, in New South Wales), the other on convictions. The meanings conveyed differ greatly. "Offenses known" signifies the number of criminal acts that come to official attention. "Convictions" signifies the number of offenders actually processed and punished. A single individual may be responsible for a large number of offenses, especially theft. The magnitudes of the two indicators thus are often vastly different: Known thefts, for example, exceed convictions by about 10:1. The amplitudes of changes in different indicators of a crime usually are different too: Known offenses tend to decrease and to increase with more volatility than arrests and convictions. But in most sets of parallel indicators we have examined, including many not reproduced here, the direction of their long-term trends is the same.[1]

TRENDS IN MURDER AND ASSAULT

Murder and serious cases of assault are more likely than any other category of common crime to receive official attention. They also are subject to relatively little definitional variation from one time and jurisdiction to another.[2] Thus a prima facie case could be made that the trends depicted in Figures II.1.1 through II.1.4 represent real changes over time in the propensity for private mayhem. Some grounds for skepticism are considered below.

In London the rates of convictions for indictable offenses for murder, manslaughter, attempted murder, and grievous assault (Figure II.1.1) were at their highest recorded levels in the 1840s. They declined between then and the 1920s by a ratio of about 8:1. The decline in attempted murder and assaults was more precipitous than the drop in murder and manslaughter. Convictions for the latter offenses, which are much less numerous, declined by a ratio of 3:1, from a high of about .70 per 100,000 population in the 1820s to .25 in the late 1920s. Comparisons for the last 50 years must be based on crimes known to the police. Reported attempts at murder and assaults (not shown in Figure II.1.1) began to rise in the 1920s and more than doubled by the late 1940s. The increase in the next 25 years, though, reduced the earlier one to insignificance: In the early 1970s Londoners were more than ten times as likely to be victimized by serious assaults as they were in the late 1940s. It is conceivable that some of this increase was due to changing police reporting procedures, but the rising rate of reported murder during these decades (see Figure II.1.1) suggests otherwise. In 1950-1951 the murder rate was .48 per 100,000, by 1971-1972 it had tripled to 1.47 per 100,000. The nineteenth century decline and the mid-twentieth century increase in indicators of aggressive crime thus have similar properties: Attempted murder and serious assaults declined, then increased simultaneously with murder, but more sharply. And the century-long decline in the murder conviction rate, by a ratio of about 3:1, was equivalent to the 1:3 increase in known murders since 1950.

London's experience of violence against persons is paralleled by that of Stockholm. (Note that since the data for Stockholm and for London are aggregated somewhat differently, the absolute rates cannot be directly compared.) In Stockholm the rate of convictions for murder, attempted murder, and manslaughter declined by a ratio of 7:1 between the 1830s and the early 1900s, though the decline is broken by a temporary doubling in the early 1880s—a period marked by numerous attacks on police and the beginnings of organized labor protest. Data on known offenses document the same long-term decline and temporary increase. The big decline between 1916 and 1917 reflects a change in recording procedures. As in London, we rely on reports rather than convictions to document the rate of mayhem thereafter.[3] The rates are consistently low through the 1920s and 1930s but begin a distinct and persistent increase around 1940. The increase in reported offenses between the 1930s and the 1960s is about 1:9, but part of the increase and subsequent decline after 1969 is a function of changes in the recording of manslaughter. No such procedural ambiguity affects the rate of reported assault (not shown graphically), which increased 500 percent between the 1940s and the early 1970s.

In New South Wales we rely on composite indicators of serious crimes against the person, including murder, manslaughter, attempted murder, and armed assault. The extraordinary nineteenth century de-

(text continued page 41)

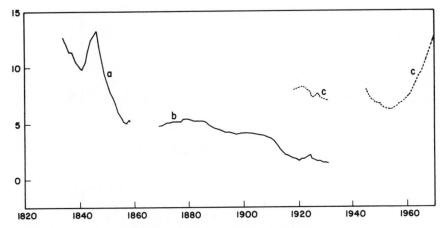

Figure II.1.1 London: Trends in murder and assault, 1834-1972

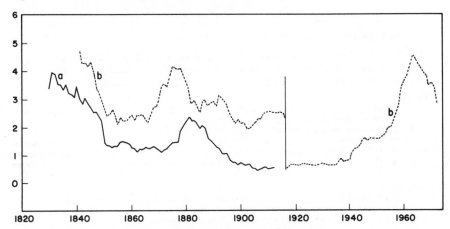

Figure II.1.2 Stockholm: Trends in murder and assault, 1830-1971

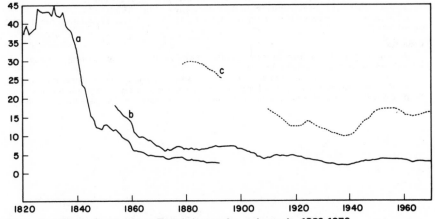

Figure II.1.3 New South Wales: Trends in murder and assault, 1820-1970

THE COMPARATIVE ANALYSIS OF PUBLIC ORDER

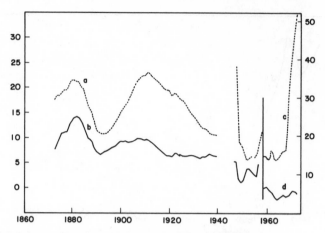

Figure II.1.4 Calcutta: Trends in murder and assault, 1873-1971

Notes to Figures on Trends in Murder and Assault

All figures show ten-year moving averages of rates per 100,000 population, except where specified. Solid lines are convictions; dashed lines are reported offenses except in New South Wales, where they signify' arrests.

London

a. Convictions for murder, manslaughter, attempted murder, and serious assaults, Middlesex County, five-year moving average, 1834-1858.

b. Convictions for same offenses as in a, MPD, 1869-1931.

c. Reported murders and manslaughter, MPD, 1918-1931, 1938, 1945-1972, per million population. Reports of all offenses in a increase so greatly after 1950 that they cannot be fitted on the same graph: the rate circa 1950 is 13 per 100,000, circa 1970 it is 90 per 100,000.

Stockholm

a. Convictions for murder, attempted murder, and manslaughter, 1830-1912.

b. Reported murders, attempted murders, and manslaughter, 1841-1971. The series is broken in 1916-1917 to reflect a change in reporting procedures.

New South Wales

a. Supreme Court convictions for serious aggressive crimes, 1820-1892.

b. All higher court convictions for serious aggressive crimes, 1854-1970.

c. Arrests for aggressive crimes against persons, 1883-1897 and 1914-1970, per 10,000 population.

Calcutta

a. Reported murders and serious assaults, 1873-1940 (ten-year moving average) and 1947-1958 (three-year moving average).

b. Convictions for murder and serious assault, same years and moving averages as in a.

c. Reported murders, 1959-1971, per million population, five-year moving average.

d. Convictions for murder, 1959-1971, per million population, five-year moving average.

cline in conviction rates is partly attributable to the declining proportion of convicts in the population, since this group was prone to violence and subject to harsh judicial sanctions. However the decline continued long after 1840, the last year that convicts were "transported" from England to New South Wales.

The index of convictions by the higher courts declined by 9:1 from the 1850s, when transportation was a fading memory, to the tranquil years of the 1930s. Another persuasive comparison is provided by the arrest and conviction rates for serious aggressive crimes between 1880s and the late 1930s: Arrests declined by a ratio of 3:1, convictions by 2:1. The postwar increase has been much less pronounced in New South Wales than in London or Stockholm, however. Arrests and higher court convictions both increased about 50 percent between 1940 and 1970, but most of the increase occurred in the first decade after the war. Reported homicides and serious assaults increased by 40 percent between 1960 and 1970. If Sydney traces the London and Stockholm pattern, steeper increases are in the offing.

The trends in murder and serious assault in Calcutta differ greatly from those of the European cities. The pattern of both recorded offenses and convictions is cyclical, with peaks in the 1880s, 1906-1915, the mid-1940s, and the early 1970s. The last three peaks coincide with periods of violent strife, generated by nationalism in the first instance, Hindu-Muslim conflict in the second, and left-right political combat in the last. The inference is that the officials knowingly included in the crime data some, perhaps all of the deaths and injuries that occurred in strife. This would also help account for the markedly greater discrepancy between offenses known and convictions between these three periods and other times: The perpetrators of murder and assault in riots are rarely caught and brought to trial. Quite a different explanation of the trends is that they reflect the extent of police activity. The ratio of police to population in Calcutta from the 1870s to 1940 traces a curve very similar to that in Figure II.1.4 (see the later chapter on "Police and Policing"). Since the Indian population of Calcutta was reluctant to report offenses to police, whom they commonly feared for their venality and brutality, it is reasonable to expect that "offenses known" depended more on the extent of police patrolling than on real trends in behavior as reflected elsewhere in citizen reports. The two explanations are complementary, not inconsistent, and we examine more evidence for them in the next section.

Distinctive long-term trends or cycles are evident in the indicators of murder and assault in all four societies. Some show tenfold decreases and increases. The second quarter of the nineteenth century and the third quarter of the twentieth were periods of intense public concern and high levels of official effort to control violent crime in the Western societies; in Calcutta four more closely spaced peaks are evident. To what extent do the indicators also reflect a changing social reality? Murders and assaults are visible and universally abhorred; thus the more serious of these offenses are likely to reach the attention of officials in any city having a rudimentary police and criminal justice system. But alternative explanations must be considered. Have police and public sensitivities about minor cases of assault changed enough over time to account for some of the trends? The sensitivity of such offenses in Western societies no doubt has increased during the last century and a half, yet for the 1800s the trend in indicators of assault was down. Moreover the 150-year trends in murder and assault are the same; both declined for a century, both increased in the last 30 years. This alternative explanation thus is not convincing; at most it may account for part of the skyrocketing increase in reported assault since 1950 in London and Stockholm.

Part of the evidence for trends in violent crime consists of conviction ratios, which may be influenced by changing judicial policies. Declining conviction ratios from the 1820s to the 1930s might be explained by arguing that judicial standards of proof have changed, making convictions on a given body of evidence decreasingly likely. The evidence against this interpretation is substantial. (a) Indicators of committals to trial (not shown here) are available for the same periods as convictions and document the same trends. (b) Where data are available on offenses known and arrests, they show the same trends as convictions. (c) The greatest expansion of defendants' rights has occurred during the last 50 years, and conviction ratios have risen, not declined, during the last part of this period. This does not rule out another possibility, though, that court jurisdictions for offenses of a given degree of seriousness have changed systematically over time. Trends in murder convictions do not admit of such an explanation; trends in assault might be more amenable. Part of the precipitous decline in convictions for crimes of violence in New South Wales between the 1820s and the 1860s, for example, is probably due to a shift of lesser offenses from the jurisdiction of the higher courts to magistrates' courts. In London summary jurisdiction over assaults was extended in 1827-1828 and again in 1926; neither had a visible effect on the rate of convictions by the higher courts. In Stockholm and Calcutta, where we have data on the activities of the lower as well as higher courts, the trends in minor assaults approximate those in serious cases.

Some of the nineteenth century decline in the indicators of violent crime in the three Western societies may be due to the altered workings of the police and courts. The same reasoning may be applicable to some of the recent increases. But not even the most skeptical multiple pleading can explain away the trends themselves. The only simple explanation that is consistent with the body of historical and statistical evidence is real change in social behavior. In these three societies, we conclude, interpersonal violence did decrease very substantially during the century that ended in the 1930s, and in London and Stockholm such behavior increased greatly in the last 30 years.

TRENDS IN THEFT

Even in the worst of times murder and assault affect only a handful of people compared to the number victimized by theft. A few statistics from London and Stockholm document the relatively high frequency of theft and thieves. In London in 1840 a total of 2,271 people were convicted for indictable crimes of robbery, burglary, larceny, and receiving stolen goods;[4] only 134 were convicted for murder and serious assault. In Stockholm in the same year 490 people were convicted for all kinds of theft compared with 75 for murder, assault, and breach of the peace. The discrepancies in reported offenses are considerably greater. In 1971 there were 266,200 indictable thefts reported in London's Metropolitan Police District, contrasted with about 8,000 murders and serious assaults (mostly the latter). The figures for Stockholm were 68,564 thefts and 2,932 cases of murder, assault, and breach of the peace. These figures are comparable within each city but not between them, because the London data are for indictable offenses only. By any standard, though, the volume of contemporary property crime is impressive: in Stockholm in 1971 there was one recorded theft for every 11 persons, in London one serious recorded theft for every 29 persons.

The social significance of the 150-year reversing trend in crimes of violence might be minimized if we could demonstrate an enduring improvement or simple persistence in trends in theft. Some comfort might even be taken from a finding that property crime has increased in lockstep with increasing prosperity. Unfortunately neither of these patterns is evident in the data on theft. In all four societies the trends and cycles are very similar to those for crimes of violence.

In London the rate of convictions for indictable (serious) crimes of theft, lines a and b in Figure II.1.5, was very high in the mid-1830s and mid-1840s but fell by a ratio of 3:1 by the beginning of the 1870s. The decline continued through the 1920s, and by the onset of the Great Depression the conviction rate was less than a tenth of what it had been a century earlier. The only reversal was a 50 percent increase between 1899 and 1908, after which the decline resumed. The trends were not identical for all forms of theft, though.

For robbery, the most serious form of theft in English law, the decline was about 7:1. Convictions for indictable larcenies declined by about 10:1. Burglary more than doubled, however, and by 1930 that crime accounted for two-thirds of all convictions for indictable theft. This changing "mix" is attributable to two factors. One was a real shift from armed robbery to burglary as the preferred method of theft, a trend that is readily explained by the progressive "disarmament" of the English citizenry and increasing penalties for crimes committed with guns. The other was officials' increased reliance, evident as early as the middle of the nineteenth century, on summary justice for larcenies that were nominally indictable. By the middle of the twentieth century virtually all larcenies, regardless of whether formally indictable, were disposed of summarily. Thus conviction trends a and b in Figure II.1.5 document a decline in the overall rate of what English officials regarded as "serious" property crimes (i.e., those worth prosecuting as indictable offenses), but they only tell us something about the changing volume of total property crime when considered in conjunction with summary convictions. Line c in Figure II.1.5 shows the trend in summary convictions for property crime between 1869 and 1931. Summary convictions were three times as numerous as indictable convictions, though they also declined between 1870 and 1930 by a ratio of about 2:1, compared with a 3:1 decline in convictions for the more serious offenses combined.

The indicator of known indictable thefts for London, beginning in 1918, shows a decade-long decline followed by a reversal that corresponds approximately with the onset of the Great Depression and continues without interruption until after World War II. The postwar improvement proved to be temporary—it lasted less than a decade. The total increase in the rate of known indictable thefts between 1935 and 1970 was about 400 percent. In 1935 there was one indictable theft reported per 120 Londoners, in 1970 there was one for every 32. The increase is not uniform across all forms of theft, any more than was the decrease. From the early 1930s to the early 1970s the robbery rate increased by 3000 percent (mostly after 1955), burglary by 700 percent, and indictable larceny by 300 percent.

The trends of theft in Stockholm (a and b in Figure II.1.6) trace a familiar pattern. Moreover they pose fewer problems of comparability or interpretation than those of London, since they represent all forms of theft and are continuously available for more than a century. Convictions per 100,000 for all thefts declined by a ratio of 5:1 between the early 1840s and the 1930s; there were sharp but temporary interruptions in the trend around 1870 and during World War I. (Sweden was a noncombatant in both world wars, but espe-

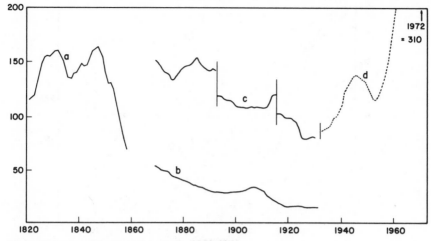

Figure II.1.5 London: Trends in theft, 1820-1972

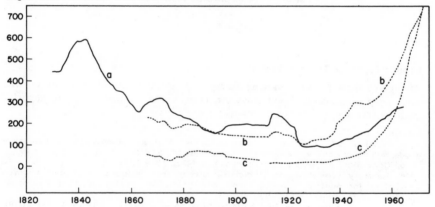

Figure II.1.6 Stockholm: Trends in theft, 1830-1971

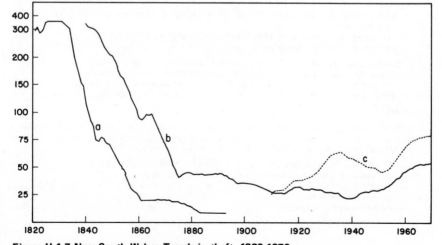

Figure II.1.7 New South Wales: Trends in theft, 1820-1970

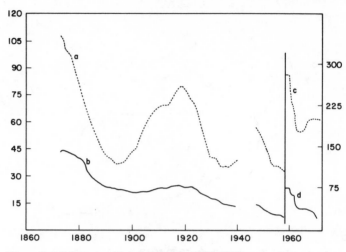

Figure II.1.8 Calcutta: Trends in theft, 1873-1971

Notes to Figures on Trends in Theft

All figures show ten-year moving averages of rates per 100,000 population, with the exceptions noted. Solid lines are convictions, dashed lines are reported offenses (arrests in New South Wales).

London
   a. Convictions for indictable offenses of robbery, burglary, larceny, and receiving stolen goods, Middlesex County, five-year moving average, 1820-1858.
   b. Convictions for indictable offenses as in a, MPD, 1869-1931.
   c. Summary convictions for indictable larceny (not included in b) plus summary convictions for nonindictable theft and similar offenses, 1869-1930. Breaks represent changes in aggregations used in 1893 and 1915.
   d. Reported offenses for indictable offenses as in a, MPD, 1933-1971, per 10,000 population.

Stockholm
   a. Convictions for all categories of theft including robbery, burglary, larceny, and pickpocketing, 1830-1963.
   b. Reported offenses as in a, 1866-1971, per 10,000 population.
   c. Reported robberies, 1866-1972.

New South Wales (Note that the vertical scale above 100 is compressed.)
   a. Supreme Court convictions for theft and similar offenses, 1820-1893.
   b. All higher court convictions for theft and similar offenses, 1840-1970.
   c. Arrests for all forms of theft, 1910-1970, per 10,000 population.

Calcutta

SOURCE: Data for 1878-1958 are from annual reports of the Calcutta commissioner of police, later data are from annual editions of **Crime in India** (New Delhi: Ministry of Home Affairs) and are not comparable in inclusiveness to earlier data.

   a. Reported noncognizable (minor) thefts, 1873-1940 and 1947-1958.
   b. Convictions for noncognizable thefts, same year as in a.
   c. Reported cognizable thefts (robbery, dacoity, burglary, ordinary theft), 1959-1971, five-year moving averages.
   d. Convictions for offenses as in c.

cially severe economic difficulties during World War I brought food riots in Stockholm, and a rise in theft.) The trend in thefts known to police per 10,000 is similar to convictions; that is, it declines irregularly from the 1860s to the mid-1920s by somewhat more than 2:1. Known thefts began to increase in the late 1930s and continued upward with scarcely any interruption into the 1970s. The 50-year increase is about 1:7. In London we observed that the more serious property crimes declined and increased more rapidly than the total volume of theft. A comparable phenomenon is evident in Stockholm:. The rate of reported robbery per 100,000 (c in Figure II.1.6) increased, especially after the 1950s, at a much more rapid rate than total theft. From 1940 to 1970 the ratio of increase was 1:20. In absolute numbers, there rarely were as many as a dozen robberies a year in Stockholm in the 1920s; in 1971 there were 615.

In New South Wales the higher court conviction rates for thefts dropped very sharply after the convict era ended. Between 1840 and 1880 they fell by a ratio of 10:1, then in the next 50 years declined by half again. The upward trend set in during World War II, and by 1970 the conviction rate had doubled. The trend in arrests for all kinds of theft, represented by line c in Figure II.1.7, shows that they have increased since 1909, with upward spurts during the Depression and after 1950. Data on known offenses are too fragmentary to trace over a long period, but they show an extraordinary rate of increase in the 1960s. Between 1960 and 1970 the rate of larceny more than doubled; breaking and entering tripled, and armed robbery increased 800 percent. In property crime, if not crimes of violence, the postwar experience of New South Wales is the same as that of London and Stockholm.

In Calcutta the trends in theft since the 1870s (Figure II.1.8) are generally similar to the city's experience of violent crime, through the 1950s. The distinct decline in known thefts and convictions from the 1870s through the 1890s may be a colonial manifestation of the processes and policies that reduced property crime in England. The subsequent increase in reported theft, though, is unique to Calcutta and coincides with the rise of the nationalist movement and a rapid expansion of the Calcutta police. There is little doubt that theft did increase during the decades after 1905: There is documentation of dramatic robberies by nationalists and looting by Moslim and Hindu rioters. But there is less reason to think that theft declined after 1920. Rather, there was a halt in police expansion and an increase in official preoccupation with the control of civil strife. We infer that the decline in reported thefts and convictions between 1920 and 1940 reflects a relative decline in police and court activity that bears no necessary relation to behavioral change. A test of this proposition is provided in Figure II.1.9, where reports of theft and convictions are calculated per policeman rather than per 100,000 population over a period of 50 years. Known thefts per policeman have the same general trends as the population-weighted trend in Figure II.1.8 but convictions per policeman do not: They steadily decline, by a ratio of about 2:1 between 1900 and the 1930s. Violent crimes per policeman show the same divergent patterns. The proposition seems to be accurate: Trends in crime indicators in Calcutta during the nationalist era were as much a function of police activity as they are of criminal behavior.[5] The data on theft after 1946 are suspect on the same grounds. Two very different series of data must be used, before and after 1958, but each shows irregular declines. The high initial level of reported theft in 1947 probably reflects the disorder that followed the riots over the partitioning of India into a Hindu state and a Moslim state. The decline thereafter, though, is almost certainly due to the diversion of official attention from common theft to more threatening problems of public order. Between 1960 and 1971 we find that common thefts known to police fall by nearly 2:1 and convictions by 4:1, whereas known robberies and dacoities (group robbery) increase by 1:4. We have observed no comparable inverse trends in any of the Western cities with respect to the forms of theft, and we regard the tendencies cited as prima facie evidence of a narrowing of the focus of official concern. Additional evidence on the general point is provided in the next chapter.

The behavioral reality of Calcutta's trends in theft is open to serious question. Is it necessary to express the same doubt regarding the three Western societies? We think not, for the same kinds of reasons that led us to infer that a changing behavioral reality underlies the trends in indicators of crimes of violence. The direction of trends in known offenses, arrests, committals to trial, and convictions are all in the same direction. So are the trends for different categories of theft, with the exception of burglary in London from 1870 to 1930. Some of the decline in higher court conviction ratios in the nineteenth century is due to a transfer of jurisdiction for petty cases from higher to lower courts. But wherever we have data on the total volume of cases of theft—in Stockholm throughout its history, in London beginning in 1869—the direction of trends is the same. The substratum of petty theft in Western societies apparently declined less than more serious forms of theft during the century of improvement, but it did decline. The rising tide of theft manifests the same internally consistent pattern: The more serious offenses have increased much more rapidly than less serious ones.

TRENDS IN WHITE-COLLAR CRIME

Theft and assault are mainly crimes of the young, the poor, and the desperate. Fraud and embezzlement are mostly crimes of middle-

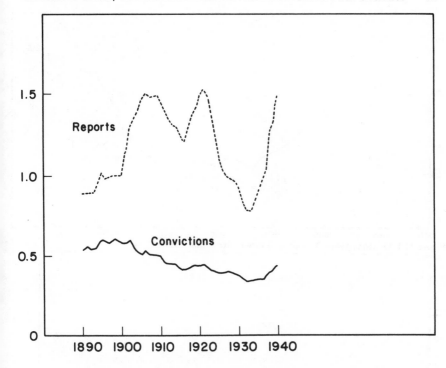

Figure II.1.9 Calcutta: Theft reports and convictions per policeman, 1890-1940, five year moving average

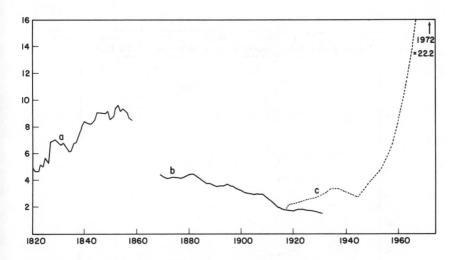

Figure II.1.10 London: Trends in white-collar crime, 1820-1972

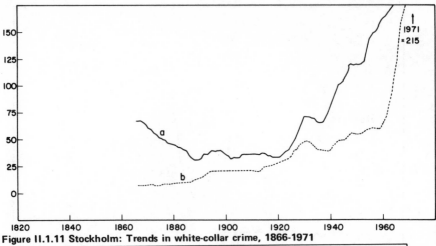

Figure II.1.11 Stockholm: Trends in white-collar crime, 1866-1971

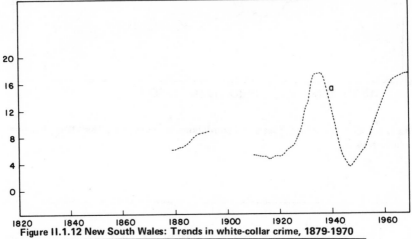

Figure II.1.12 New South Wales: Trends in white-collar crime, 1879-1970

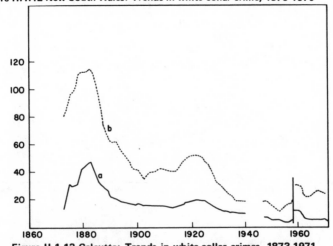

Figure II.1.13 Calcutta: Trends in white-collar crimes, 1873-1971

Notes to Figures on Trends in White-Collar Crime

All figures show ten-year moving averages of rates per 100,000 population, with the exceptions nóted. Solid lines are convictions, dashed lines are reported offenses (arrests in New South Wales).

London
    a. Convictions for indictable fraud and embezzlement, Middlesex County, five-year moving average, 1820-1858.
    b. Convictions for indictable fraud and embezzlement, MPD, 1869-1931.
    c. Reported cases of fraud and embezzlement, MPD, 1918-1972.

Stockholm
    a. Convictions for fraud, embezzlement, forgery, and offenses by officials, 1866-1964.
    b. Reported cases of fraud, embezzlement, and forgery per 10,000, 1866-1971.

New South Wales
    Arrests for fraud, embezzlement, forgery, and similar offenses, 1879-1893, 1910-1970.

Calcutta
SOURCE: Data for 1878-1958 are from annual reports of the Calcutta commissioner of police, later data are from annual editions of **Crime in India** (New Delhi: Ministry of Home Affairs) and are not necessarily comparable to earlier data.
    a. Convictions for cognizable (serious) cheating, breach of trust, counterfeiting, and similar offenses, 1873-1940, 1947-1958 (three-year moving average), 1959-1971 (five-year moving average).
    b. Reported cases of cognizable offenses, as in a.

class employees and business men. Theft and white-collar crime are motivated by avarice, but the embezzler has the advantages of skills and opportunities of a different order from those of the common thief. Since the class position and opportunities of thieves differ markedly from those of white-collar criminals, we might expect the social dynamics of white-collar crime to be different and its trends to differ as a consequence.

The trends in indicators of white-collar crime in London (Figure II.1.10) prove to be familiar. Conviction rates are highest in the 1840s and 1850s; from 1870 to 1930 they decline gradually but consistently by a ratio of about 3:1. Known offenses increase by about 50 percent between the two wars; after 1945 they increase more rapidly, by 700 percent as of 1972. The only significant difference between these trends and those for theft is the trend from 1820 to 1858, when the rate of convictions for white-collar offenses nearly doubled. This probably reflects the rapid expansion of commercial enterprise in London during the first half of the nineteenth century, hence an equally rapid expansion in opportunities for white-collar crime.

The nineteenth century Stockholm data (Figure II.1.11) show a 2:1 decline in convictions for white-collar crime during the last third of the nineteenth century followed by several decades of little change. A rapid increase begins in the 1920s, about a decade earlier than the turning point for common theft. The rate of convictions increases by 600 percent in the next 40 years. Offenses known show a steady, gradual increase from the 1860s onward. The ratio of increase between the 1860s and the 1920s is 1:4. In the next 50 years the offenses increase by another 700 percent. The evidence from Stockholm thus is ambiguous about whether a decline in white-collar crime occurred during the nineteenth century: Convictions declined, known offenses increased. An "opportunity" explanation best fits the data. Large-scale commercial development did not begin in Stockholm until the last decades of the nineteenth century; before that opportunities for fraud were fewer and offenders more easily detected. The twentieth century increase in known offenses and convictions can be attributed to the rapid expansion of opportunities and commensurate official efforts at control.

White-collar crime in New South Wales apparently has been cyclical, on the basis of the fragmentary arrest data in Figure II.1.12. During the Depression arrests increased by 400 percent, and a 400 percent increase following World War II substantially outstripped the simultaneous 200 percent increase in common theft.

In Calcutta the long-term trend in white-collar crime from the 1880s to the 1970s has been irregularly but consistently downward (Figure II.1.13). The indicators are aggregated from a diverse set of offenses such as forgery, cheating, use of false weights and measurements, and giving false evidence. The noticeable increase from about 1915 to 1925 coincides with a much greater increase in common theft, but the interpretation is ambiguous. Since policing had increased in previous years, the apparent rise in white-collar crime is probably due less to behavior change than to better reporting. The subsequent decline almost surely reflects a decline in policing. The beginnings of Calcutta's commercial decline, which can be seen in the 1930s, surely were not yet sufficient to restrict the opportunities for fraudulent activities.

In the Western societies the opportunities for white-collar crime have increased as a function of economic growth generally and commercial expansion specifically. We suspect that the trends depicted in Figures II.1.10 to II.1.12 provide a somewhat distorted version of an underlying behavioral reality. The "century of improvement" in public order had the effect of keeping white-collar crime at relatively low levels despite the expansion of opportunities. The Depression that began in the late 1920s was a strong inducement to hard-pressed members of the middle class to bend and break the economic rules. By no means all sharp commercial practices are illegal, and only some of the illegal ones led to convictions. Thus when it was perceived that breaking the rules contributed to the economic betterment of those who did so, more and more people began to take advantage of the ample opportunities available in expanding urban economies. The hypothesis—we have no direct evidence for it—is that practices that caught hold during times of austerity were so successful that they were widely imitated during the subsequent periods of prosperity. They may even have provided cues that helped stimulate the dramatic increases in common theft.

THE REGULATION OF SOCIAL CONDUCT

Many kinds of deviant social conduct have been treated as crimes in Western societies. Some, like adultery and drunkenness, are so common that they are not "deviant" at all but are regulated nonetheless. A sketch of the criminalization and decriminalization of different kinds of social conduct is offered in a later chapter. Here we examine the evidence of trends in the public regulation of sexual conduct and the consumption of alcohol. It is unreasonable to expect trends in indicators of these offenses to correspond to a changing behavioral reality. Patterns of sexual behavior and alcohol consumption obviously have changed over time, but the amount of official attention given them has changed even more, and there is no warrant for assuming that the two kinds of change are correlative. The trends examined here are, first and foremost, reflections of change in official interests and policies.

Rather different kinds of sexual conduct have been regulated in Western societies.[6] The indicators in Figures II.1.14 through II.1.16 represent a mixed bag of offenses ranging from rape and homosexual acts to indecent exposure—often an official euphemism for public urination. The evidence of the conviction ratios suggests that the regulation of these offenses is cyclical. Both the London and New South Wales data include convictions for only the most serious offenses. In London the conviction ratio peaks in the 1830s, a time of intense concern about theft and violence as well; a spillover effect may have been at work. Convictions for sex crimes increased dramatically between 1880 and 1900 without a corresponding rise in conviction rates for other offenses, and it is tempting to interpret this as an official manifestation of Victorian morality. In New South Wales there appear to be localized peaks in convictions at the same two periods: in the 1830s and around 1890. The same interpretations are applicable. The first corresponds with the extremely high levels of official action against theft and violence, the second signifies the judicial response to vociferous public and legislative concern about sex crimes, amply documented in our study of public order in New South Wales.[7]

The conviction data for Stockholm are more difficult to interpret because the kinds of offenses included are not specified. Evidently minor offenses as well as more serious ones are incorporated. The decided downward trend in convictions from the 1890s through the 1930s is consistent with what we know of the history of decriminalization of sexual offenses in Sweden. A separate series of data on convictions for adultery, not included in Figure II.1.15, shows that these too declined markedly during the latter part of the nineteenth century; the last conviction for adultery in Stockholm was in 1917. Data on sexual offenses known trace quite a different pattern, though; they rise in the late nineteenth century, then decline into the early 1920s. We know only that these are "gross sexual offenses," that is, offenses more serious than those represented by the declining trend in convictions.

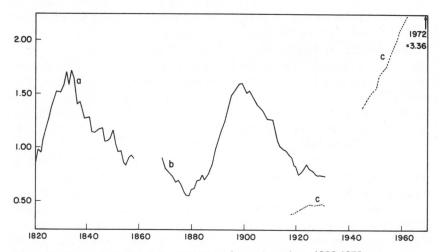

Figure II.1.14 London: Trends in regulation of sexual conduct, 1820-1972

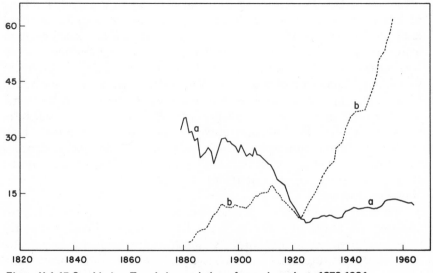

Figure II.1.15 Stockholm: Trends in regulation of sexual conduct, 1879-1964

All three societies show evidence of rising concern about sexual offenses during the past 40 to 50 years. Offenses recorded by police began to increase in the 1920s in London and Stockholm; arrests in New South Wales rise after 1940. Convictions increase slightly in Stockholm and very substantially in New South Wales. Social histories provide considerable documentation of the changing sexual mores of Western societies during this period. The rising trend in known offenses and arrests through the 1950s thus reflects both the growing diversity of sexual conduct and the fact that official criteria

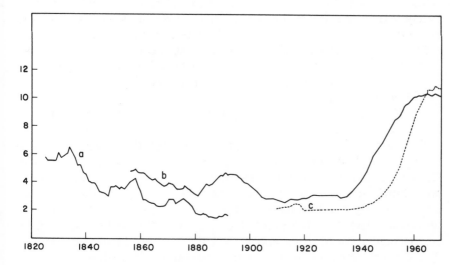

Figure II.1.16 New South Wales: Trends in regulation of sexual conduct, 1825-1970

Notes to Figures on Regulation of Sexual Conduct

All figures show ten-year moving averages of rates per 100,000 population, with the exceptions noted. Solid lines are convictions, dashed lines are reported offenses (arrests in New South Wales).

London

 a. Convictions for indictable rapes and attempts, homosexual acts and attempts, indecent exposure, and similar offenses, Middlesex County, five-year moving average, 1820-1858.

 b. Convictions for indictable offenses as in a, MPD, 1869-1931.

 c. Reported offenses as in a, MPD, 1918-1931, 1938, 1945-1972, per 10,000 population.

Stockholm

 a. Convictions for indecent behavior and similar sexual offenses, 1879-1964. Specific kinds of offenses are not identified in the sources.

 b. Reported gross sexual offenses, including rape, 1882-1967. Specific kinds of offenses are not identified in the sources before 1952, but the aggregation is less inclusive than in a.

New South Wales

 a. Supreme Court convictions for rape and attempts, homosexual acts and attempts, bestiality, bigamy, and similar offenses, 1825-1896.

 b. Higher court convictions for offenses as in a, 1857-1970.

 c. Arrests for all sexual offenses, 1910-1970, per 20,000 population.

of sexual criminality had not yet adapted to changing social standards. In the 1960s in Stockholm and New South Wales all the indicators appear to have peaked out (unlike the indicators of assault and theft), suggesting that official standards were being modified. We know from our detailed studies that this period was characterized by formal decriminalization and informal relaxation of enforcement.

The mood of toleration of sexual diversity has limits, however. Rape and other kinds of sexual assault are not on the verge of being decriminalized in any Western society. The incidence of these offenses has increased in recent decades at a rate comparable to other sexual offenses: In Stockholm the increase in reported rapes was 300 percent between 1951 and 1971, in New South Wales it was 200 percent between 1960 and 1970. The decriminalization of benign offenses like homosexuality and the use of mild narcotics may facilitate official efforts at controlling the kinds of sexual attacks that continue to be universally condemned in Western societies.

Public drunkenness provides a larger volume of police business in most Western societies than any other nontraffic offense. In Stockholm in 1910 about 80 percent of all sentences meted out by the courts were for drunkenness, and in 1960 the figure was about 70 percent. In New South Wales 50 percent of all nontraffic arrests in the late 1940s were for drunkenness; 20 years later the proportion was about one-third. In London during the last century, drunkenness and disorderly conduct has been the occasion for 30 to 45 percent of all arrests. The data in Figures II.1.17 to II.1.19 reveal the variability of the regulation of drunkenness over the long run in all three places. The highest rates are recorded in Stockholm, where the conviction rate in the first decade of this century reached a peak of 4,100 per 100,000. Since virtually all the guilty were adult males, this means that about one man in eight was convicted of the offense each year, though no doubt there were many repeaters. The rate of nineteenth century increase in sentences for drunkenness in Stockholm is also misleading about the actual incidence of the offense. The sixfold, 60 year increase from the 1840s to 1910 is an official testimonial to the influence of the temperance movement. The trends in the last 60 years, though, trace with some accuracy the changing availability of beer and aquavit. The sharp decline in sentences after 1910 coincides with the imposition of strict rationing policies. Rationing ended in 1955, and public drunkenness apparently tripled.

In London arrests for drunkenness have been proportionally fewer than in Stockholm and New South Wales, except during the 1830s when arrests annually exceeded 2,000 per 100,000 population. Enforcement appears to have been episodic, with 10- to twenty-year periods of intensified enforcement around 1850, in the 1870s, and from the 1890s to World War I. The new licensing laws may help account for the low arrest rates during the decades between wars, and relaxed standards of police enforcement may have contributed to this effect. Since 1945 there has been a steady increase in arrests, by 300 percent in three decades. The upward movement has been so consistent that it is more likely to be due to real change in public behavior than to differences in police enforcement.

In New South Wales arrests for drunkenness also have varied cyclically. The peaks in the 1880s and the late 1940s correspond with periods of public concern and stepped-up police enforcement. Whether these episodes reflect behavioral change as well is unknowable. The most recent peak began almost immediately after the end of World War II, and it is at least plausible that the increase in drunkenness arrests, along with the simultaneous rise in arrests for assault, reflects official efforts to control the activities of discharged servicemen.

THE COMMON TRENDS IN COMMON CRIME IN WESTERN SOCIETIES

Though lacking crime indicators to reinforce or undermine their perceptions, the articulate people who lived through the 1830s and 1840s in London, Stockholm, and Sydney left ample testimony in their writings and in the policies they pursued of their conviction that they lived in dangerous times. Their descendants, however, became increasingly certain of the security of their persons and property in the course of the next three generations. Virtually every

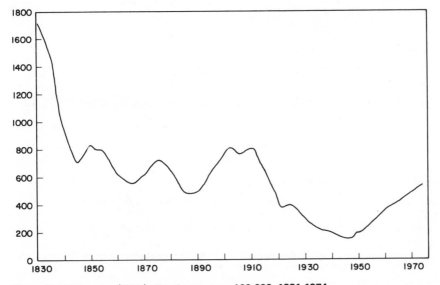

Figure II.1.17 London (MPD): Drunkenness per 100,000, 1831-1974

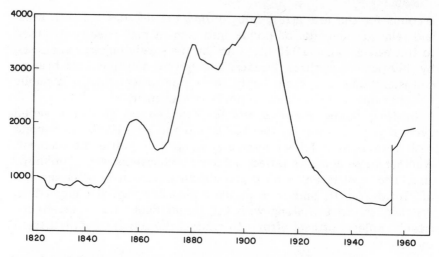

Figure II.1.18 Stockholm: Trends in regulation of alcohol abuse, 1822-1964

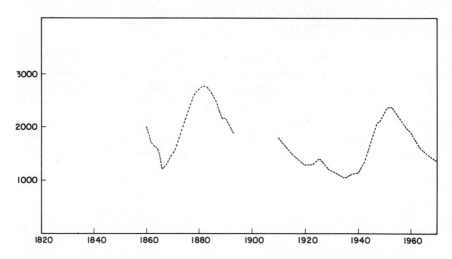

Figure II.1.19 New South Wales: Trends in regulation of alcohol abuse, 1820-1970

Notes to Figures on Regulation of Alcohol Abuse

All figures show ten-year moving averages of rates per 100,000 population.

London
    Persons arrested for drunkenness and disorderly conduct, 1831-1974.

Stockholm
    Persons sentenced for drunkenness, 1822-1964. The series is broken in 1955-1956 to show the impact of the end of liquor rationing in 1955.

New South Wales
    Persons arrested for drunkenness, 1859-1893, 1910-1970.

indicator we have examined, whether of police or court activity, of theft or assault, of serious or petty offenses, testifies to the social reality of improving public order during the latter half of the nineteenth century and the early decades of the twentieth century.

The downward trends in crimes of violence and theft among the three Western cities are similar enough to be plotted on a single graph (Figure II.1.20) representing the relative decline in convictions for crimes of violence and theft. The decline from eight around 1840 to just over one in 1930 signifies that the conviction rates declined, on the average, by a ratio of 8:1. In New South Wales, for example, in the early 1850s the higher courts convicted about eighteen persons per 100,000 population of murder or grievous assault, whereas in the early 1930s only about two per 100,000 were convicted. The 9:1 decline in New South Wales was slightly higher than the average; the vertical bars represent the range of variation around the common trend.[8]

The reversal in the common trend begins in the late 1930s. The timing was somewhat different among societies; in some it was detectable as early as 1930, in others not until 1945. By the mid-1960s the conviction rates had increased, on the average, more than 100 percent from their low point between the wars and were at about the same level they had reached at the turn of the century.

The fateful question is what these trends signify. In the conventional or "official" view they are a direct reflection of changes in criminal behavior, which are shown here to be common to three cities. But conviction data present at best a diffracted image of social behavior that has passed through the distorting lenses of differential public concern, selective reporting and enforcement, and bureaucratic processing. Then we must ask whether the trends are due to changes in the institutions of public order. They cannot be attributed to the changing scope of criminal law because, as we show in a later chapter, there has been little substantive change in legal definitions of offenses against persons and property. The century-long decline in the conviction rates cannot by any stretch of the imagination be attributed to declining police efficiency. Instead the decline coincides with the establishment of effective, centralized police forces in all three cities. A third possibility is that the judicial disposition of cases has shifted. To the extent that offenders are dealt with summarily, they do not appear in data on convictions in serious crimes. Historical evidence suggests that some of the decline in conviction ratios in London and New South Wales can be attributed to a shift of jurisdiction of cases from higher to lower courts. But wherever we have data on convictions for all offenses, serious and petty (in Stockholm for 130 years, in London for shorter periods), the decline is less pronounced but the same trends are evident. It seems that only a small part of the reversing trend in conviction rates is due to institutional change. The inference is that the changing conviction ratios trace approximately, the institutional response to changing patterns of social behavior.

Trends in the courts' disposition to convict are less persuasive as evidence of social change than are trends in offenses known, because the latter are based on the reports of police and citizens who are most likely to know firsthand about the incidence of assault and theft. Their reports are not widely available until after 1900. During the 60 years across which we can trace them for all three societies (Figure II.1.21) they show the same trends as the conviction data. There are only two differences. One is that the offenses known begin to increase in the late 1920s, a decade before the reversal of the trend in convictions. The second, and more significant, is that known offenses fell more rapidly than convictions during the last of the era of improvement and accelerated much more rapidly after 1950.

Part of the recent increase in known crime might be a function of two social facts: People in contemporary Western societies have access to telephones, an easy means of reporting offenses to the police, and the prospect of insurance claims is an added incentive to make known losses, especially serious ones. Positive feedback also

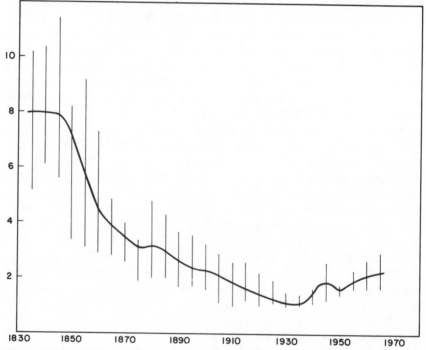

Figure II.1.20 The common trend in convictions for crimes of theft and violence in Western societies, 1835-1965

may be at work. Crime reports are grist for newspaper accounts and indicators of rising crime, which reinforce the common perception that we live in disorderly times. The effect may be to encourage people to report offenses, especially petty ones, that earlier might not have been reported. Or, equally plausible, increased awareness of crime may breed public cynicism, which reduces the disposition to report small losses that are not covered by insurance. Another possibility is that police today are less selective in reporting offenses than previously. Systematic changes of this type are easily detected, though. Modifications in London in 1931 and in New South Wales in 1970 caused step-level increases in recorded crime which are readily distinguishable from the cumulative, year-by-year increases that characterize the three cities in this study since the 1950s.

Some but not much of the average fivefold increase in known assaults and thefts during the past 40 years may be explained by a growing disposition to report offenses. Murders have increased as well as assaults. Reports of the more serious forms of theft have increased much more rapidly than indicators of petty theft. White-collar crime and serious sexual offenses, especially rape, have escalated at the same rapid rates. Victimization studies show a large reservoir of unreported offenses even in the late 1960s and early 1970s; it is scarcely likely that the reservoir would be so large if it had been the source of reports that had already increased by multiples of 3, 5, 10, and 20. We suspect, in fact, that crime indicators understate the true rate of increase in minor theft in recent decades. Cynicism is one reason; another is growing prosperity, which makes a

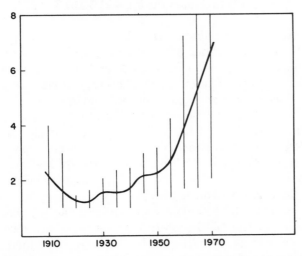

Figure II.1.21 The common trend in known crimes of theft and violence in Western societies, 1910-1970

small loss scarcely worth reporting. If this is true, it helps explain both the large "dark figure" (the European term for unreported crimes) revealed in recent victimization surveys and the fact that serious theft reportedly has increased more than petty offenses. We conclude that social behavior obviously has changed in these societies in the last 30 to 40 years, and although the crime indicators may reflect those changes in a distorted way, they reflect it nonetheless.

Reversing trends in public order have proved to be remarkably similar across three different and distant cities. Other studies of long-term trends in common crime provide evidence that this reversal is by no means unique to the cases investigated. The nineteenth century trends in conviction rates for London are paralleled by the data for all England and Wales: committals to trial for all serious offenses increased from 1805 to the 1840s by a ratio of about 1:4 but declined by 3:1 during the next 50 years. The trends, though not these precise ratios, characterize both property crime and crimes against the person. Gatrell and Hadden attribute part of the increase in the first part of the century to institutional changes, but they conclude that the subsequent decline probably understates the true reduction in criminal activity.[9] In France the rate of persons accused of property crime declined by a ratio of 10:1 between 1826 and the 1930s and remained relatively low until the 1950s. Crimes of violence fluctuated over this period without any clear trend.[10] Our examination of recent French data shows a doubling in property crime rates between 1955 and 1970. A study of crime in Canada from 1901 to 1960 gives contrasting results: Crimes against property nearly tripled, and offenses against persons increased 800 percent, with particularly sharp increases during 1910-1915, 1935-1939, and 1955-1960.[11]

National trends in crime rates are not necessarily the same as those in cities, however. A number of cities in the United States, but few elsewhere, have undergone such studies, and most of them exhibit trends similar to those of London, Stockholm, and New South Wales. Studies of Boston reveal a pronounced decline in indicators of various kinds of serious crime between the middle of the nineteenth century and the 1930s or 1940s.[12] A study of Buffalo, N.Y., from 1856 to 1946 shows that known crimes against persons and property peaked around 1870 and declined irregularly thereafter. By 1946 violent crimes were down by a ratio of 5:1, property crimes by only 1.5:1.[13] A final comparison is provided by a century of arrest data for Chicago (Figure II.1.22). There was an irregular 4:1 decline from the 1870s through the 1940s, interrupted by two sharp reversals, the second one coinciding with the Prohibition era. The increase from 1950 to 1970 was about 300 percent.[14] Similar increases in crime indicators in almost all American cities after 1950 are well known and they need no documentation here.[15]

The reversing 140-year trend in indicators of crimes against persons and property in London, Stockholm, and New South Wales reflects profound changes in public concern about threatening social behavior and official efforts to control it. Real changes in social behavior evidently underlay altered perceptions of public disorder, though the indicators probably exaggerate the nineteenth century decline in assault and theft and understate the recent increase in

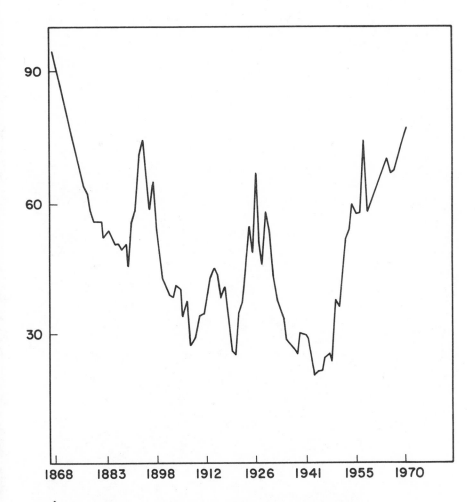

Figure II.1.22 Chicago: Total arrests per 1,000 population, 1868-1970

theft. In Calcutta the trends in crime indicators permit few firm inferences about changing patterns of individual behavior. Most of the fluctuations noted are due to changes in the scope of official efforts at social control and to the impact of civil strife.

NOTES TO PART II, CHAPTER 1

1. Annual data on general and more specific categories of offenses are portrayed in the city studies, published separately, as are some of the statistics on arrests and trials.

2. Dr. S. Mukherjee of the United Nations Social Defense Research Institute, in Rome, has made a systematic, unpublished study of the formal definitions of murder, manslaughter, and similar offenses in nineteen countries, representing all world regions. The elements of the definitions prove to be closely comparable.

3. Data on convictions for murderous offenses are available in Stockholm through 1951 but are not comparable with earlier data because they include, without separate tabulation, sentences for procuring abortions. The aggregation is instructive about changing Swedish values (since 1975 abortion has been legal under almost all circumstances) but not about the changing incidence of convictions for murderous assault.

4. In the lexicon of crime in English-speaking countries, robbery is the most serious form of theft and involves the use or threat of force against the victim. Burglary involves surreptitious entry, usually into homes or commercial establishments. Larcency is the theft of property from public places (e.g., bicycle theft and shoplifting). One or more classes of larceny are typically distinguished (grand vs. petty, indictable vs. summary, etc.), based on the value of goods stolen. The aggregate measures of theft used in our analyses also include a variety of less numerous theft-related offenses such as attempted robbery and burglary, receiving stolen goods, and pickpocketing.

5. This proposition applies only to Calcutta. The Western cities experienced several periods, identified in the later chapter on police and policing, during which increased policing led to rising crime rates, but these are short-term phenomena and are not comparable to the enduring pattern in Calcutta.

6. Sexual offenses and drunkenness were so rarely recorded in Calcutta that little is to be gained by examining the statistics. What is significant is that neither British nor Indian officials though it necessary to police these activities.

7. See also Peter N. Grabosky, *Sydney in Ferment: Crime, Dissent, and Official Reaction, 1788-1973* (Canberra: Australian National University Press, 1976).

8. This is the procedure used to determine the common trend in Figures II.1.20 and II.1.21. For each city, the moving ten-year average for convictions was recorded for every fifth year for which data were available (as shown in Figures II.1.1 through II.1.7): for 1830, 1835, 1840, and so forth. The lowest rate in each series was set equal to 1.0 and the other rates expressed as a ratio of that one. In London, for example, the lowest average conviction rate recorded for indictable murders and assaults between 1820 and 1930 was 1.36 per 100,000 in 1930, the highest was 12.5 in 1845. The 1930 ratio was set at 1.0; the 1845 ratio therefore was 12.5 ÷ 1.36 = 9.2. The procedure was repeated for the trend in indictable thefts, and for both kinds of convictions in New South Wales (higher court convictions) and Stockholm (all convictions). Since all the series have a common minimum of 1.0, they can be plotted on the same graph. The graph covers only the period for which at least four ratios were available. New South Wales is excluded before 1850 because of its exceptionally high rates

during the convict era; if these data were included, the 1830s average would exceed 10. The vertical bars represent the range of variation around the mean. In 1880, for example, the highest ratio score was 4.8 (aggressive crimes in Stockholm), the lowest was 2.0 (theft in New South Wales), the average of six ratios was 3.2. Neither kind of offense and no one city has a consistently higher or lower rate of decline.

9. V. A. C. Gatrell and T. B. Hadden, "Criminal Statistics and Their Interpretation," in E. A. Wrigley (ed.), op. cit., pp. 372-379.

10. Lodhi and Tilly, op. cit.

11. P. J. Giffen, "Rates of Crime and Delinquency," in W. T. McGrath, ed., Crime and Its Treatment in Canada (New York: St. Martin's Press, 1965), ch. 4.

12. Sam Bass Warner, Crime and Criminal Statistics. in Boston (Cambridge: Harvard University Press, 1934); Theodore N. Ferdinand, "The Criminal Patterns of Boston Since 1849," American Journal of Sociology, 73 (July 1967), 688-698; Roger Lane, Policing the City: Boston, 1822-1885 (Cambridge: Harvard University Press, 1967); Roger Lane, "Urbanization and Criminal Violence in the 19th Century: Massachusetts as a Test Case," in H. D. Graham and T. R. Gurr, eds., Violence in America, ch. 12.

13. Elwin H. Powell, The Design of Discord: Studies of Anomie (New York: Oxford University Press, 1970), ch. 8.

14. From Wesley G. Skogan, Chicago Since 1840: A Time-Series Data Handbook (Urbana: Institute of Government and Public Affairs, University of Illinois, 1975).

15. See Fred P. Graham, "A Contemporary History of American Crime," in Graham and Gurr, eds., op. cit., ch. 13, for national data. For a comparison of data for all the large American cities see Wesley G. Skogan, "Law, Order, and the Transformation of Urban Society," paper presented to the Midwest Political Science Association, Chicago, 1974.

Chapter 2

CIVIL STRIFE AND CRISES OF PUBLIC ORDER

Our assessment of trends in crime has relied mainly on indicators of the official attention given to crimes and criminals. Civil strife leaves more substantial tracings in the journalistic and historical accounts of its time. A review of narrative and official evidence about the incidence of strife in the four cities provides the basis for a comparative interpretation of changing magnitudes, issues, tactics, and forms of group conflict. In the second part of the chapter we juxtapose the evidence about short-run increases in official data on common crime and episodes of civil strife and demonstrate that these phenomena coincide with remarkable frequency.

TRENDS IN CIVIL STRIFE

The Historical Record

The cities differ widely in the timing, circumstances, and severity of civil conflict.

Calcutta: Undoubtedly Calcutta has been the most turbulent of the four cities in the twentieth century, but its nineteenth century history contains very few references to serious episodes of protest or rebellion. Most collective disorder in Bengal before 1905 occurred away from Calcutta. Traditional Islamic resistance to British rule in the early nineteenth century had few urban manifestations. Colonial forces made strenuous efforts to control thugism and dacoity, which were rife in the rural areas of Bengal, but these murderous forms of banditry came no closer to the city than the nearby riverways.

Peasant revolts in the 1850s had even less impact on public order in Calcutta, and the Sepoy Mutiny of 1857 had none at all.

The first serious strife in Calcutta proper was distinctly modern in purpose and form: It was a manifestation of Bengali nationalism, which had begun as an intellectual and social movement among urban middle-class Hindus in the 1820s. Polite opposition to British policies throughout the century gave way gradually to mass agitational politics. The first episodes occurred in the 1880s but were infrequent and limited in scope; in 1905, however, British plans to partition Bengal stimulated the first wave of the widespread nationalist resistance that was to continue until independence. During those years strife took every form conceivable in an urban setting, including boycotts, strikes, protracted terrorism, massive demonstrations, and large-scale riots. The peaks of nationalist activity in Calcutta occurred at intervals of roughly a decade: 1906-1908, 1912-1915, 1920-1924, 1930-1934, and 1942-1946. It is noteworthy that serious communal conflict between Hindus and Muslims followed rather than preceded the onset of militant nationalism and was exacerbated by the growing schism in the political sympathies of the two groups: Many Muslim leaders were co-opted into the apparatus of colonial rule, most Hindus opposed it. Communal strife was chronic after the first major episode of communal violence in 1918, and there were particularly virulent outbreaks in 1926 and in 1946, the single most bloody year in Calcutta's history. Strikes over economic issues did not become common until the early 1920s, but they too soon took on a political cast.

A crescendo of political, communal, and labor violence speeded Britain's formal withdrawal in 1947 from a province and a city she no longer controlled. But independence failed to resolve hostilities that had been exacerbated by decades of conflict between radical and conservative politicians, Hindus and Muslims, workers and employers. Quite the contrary: The success of protest and rebellion as means to independence appears to have increased the attractiveness of these activities to antagonistic groups. Since most of the radical nationalists were excluded from the postindependence governments of Calcutta and West Bengal, they continued open rebellion and sporadic campaigns of terrorism and sabotage for some years, though with declining amplitude until the onset of Naxalite terrorism in the late 1960s. The most durable tradition has proved to be mass agitation. Every divisive political, economic, and communal issue in Calcutta's postwar history has been marked by rallies, strikes, demonstrations, and riots that have become what might well be called an "alternative urban lifestyle."

Stockholm: The Swedish city reverses the Calcutta pattern. Its history between 1700 and 1900 was rather tumultuous, albeit on the small scale to be expected in a small city, but for most of the past 50 years it has been notably free of civil strife. In the earlier period strife had two quite different components: Stockholm was the arena in which national political conflicts were fought out, and it also had a fractious citizenry given to spontaneous street protest and fighting inspired by the sociochemical interaction of group antagonisms and aquavit. Strife focusing on unpopular soldiers or police, without specific ideological content, was particularly common during the late 1780s and 1790s, and again from the 1860s through the 1890s.

Explicitly political conflict evolved through three stages, each characterized by substantial strife. Struggles between the monarchy and nobility were manifest in coups of 1772, 1789, and 1809, and the assassination of King Gustav III in 1792. The political interests of the growing middle and artisan classes fueled serious political riots in 1809, 1838, and 1848. Working-class demands were evident in the events of 1848, but significant organized strife by the working class did not develop until the 1890s, when workers initiated frequent strikes and demonstrations aimed at resolving economic issues and securing the franchise. These issues were the source of much open conflict that continued into the second decade of the twentieth century.

Issues of class political and economic conflict were largely resolved by the early 1920s. The years of World War I were turbulent in Stockholm, though, first because of demonstrations for and against Swedish neutrality, and later because of strikes and riots inspired by severe economic depression, occasioned by the wartime disruption of trade. Since the 1920s strife in Stockholm has taken the form of substantial strike activity in 1924-1925, 1932, and 1952; demonstrations against American involvement in Southeast Asia in the late 1960s and early 1970s; and occasional apolitical street clashes. Demonstrations have been by far the most numerous of these events: Swedish sources indicate that some 260 occurred in Stockholm between 1961 and 1970. Virtually all demonstrations had foreign not domestic political objects, and few were disruptive. The most substantial issue of domestic political protest in Stockholm in recent years, in fact, seems to have been opposition to removal of a stand of elm trees. On this issue, as in many others in Sweden's history, the protestors ultimately won the day.

London: Apparently London experienced in the nineteenth century conflict as widespread as that of Stockholm, but less violent. In the twentieth century London has had strife of greater magnitude and seriousness. The heyday of the "London mob" was in the eighteenth century; by the nineteenth century the urban proletariat was unorganized and usually quiescent. No popular support was attracted by the Cato Street conspirators, for example, who attempted a revolutionary seizure of power in London in 1816 and plotted another in 1820. The great movements for political reform of the nineteenth century included agitation over the first Reform Bill in 1830-1832, the Chartist movement from 1835 to 1848, and the demonstrations over the Second Reform Bill in 1865-1867. The major support for the first two causes came from outside London, and when the London workers did participate in rallies and demonstrations on behalf of reform they were almost always peaceable and careful to avoid potentially violent confrontations. Nonetheless the English elite greatly feared rebellion during the first half of the century and responded to popular protest by employing a network of spies and informers, massive shows of force, and harsh judicial sanctions. The cautious tactics of London protestors also characterized the labor movement. London was affected by fairly widespread strikes in 1859-1861 (in the building trades), in 1888 (among dock workers), in the years immediately before and after World War I, and in 1926—the year of the nationwide general strike; but on the whole the tenor of labor disputes in London was peaceful, one is tempted to say deferential.

Parallel to the activities of organized labor, a vociferous socialist movement emerged in the last quarter of the nineteenth century. The socialists' favorite public activities were outdoor rallies and processions, events they organized in substantial number over a period of many years. In times of economic distress these occasions were sometimes disruptive, but as a rule they were all of a piece with the tradition of orderly protest that has inspired hundreds of demonstrations a year in London—the war years excepted—over almost every domestic and international issue imaginable. The most threatening manifestations of strife in London during the latter part of the nineteenth century were episodes of Fenian terrorist activity, which continued sporadically in the twentieth century.

The last battles in the campaign for universal suffrage were fought by the feminists between 1900 and 1914. The militant suffragettes, mainly a middle-class group, were neither deferential nor afraid to employ violent tactics. The streets of London were their principal battleground, and they made calculated and dramatized use of mass demonstrations, physical confrontations with police, and campaigns of arson, bombing, and the kind of property destruction lately called "trashing." Suffrage was extended to women in 1918, after a wartime suspension of domestic hostilities, and the decades of the 1920s and the 1940s were largely free of group conflict in London. In the 1930s, however, the activities of Sir Oswald Mosley's British Union of Fascists were a serious threat to public order, mainly because of their success in provoking their many opponents into brawls.

Since the mid-1950s civil strife in London has increased markedly. The increase has four dimensions, all manifestations of national problems. One is labor conflict, which has grown significantly during each period of Conservative government and has contributed to the early demise of one of those governments. Second is the rise of civil disobedience, which began with the "Ban the Bomb" movement of the 1960s and spilled over into protest against the Vietnam war and a variety of other international issues in which Britain was scarcely implicated. The third is ethnic conflict, observable in recurring small-scale attacks on nonwhite immigrants from the Commonwealth—and, most recently, attacks by black youths on white police. Last is the rise in the 1970s of protest and terrorist violence by or on behalf of Irish nationalists. The protagonists in these conflicts have few interests or tactics in common, but their cumulative effect has been to make contemporary London the most strife-ridden of the Western cities in this study.

New South Wales: This Australian state deserves the sobriquet of "quiescent polity,"[1] thanks to a remarkably strife-free history since its founding in 1788. Virtually the only episodes of strife in nineteenth century Sydney before the rise of the labor movement were a revolt of Irish convicts in 1804 and a few "issueless riots" in the 1840s and 1860s. Workers demonstrated against immigration of Chinese in the 1880s and organized some substantial strikes, notably in 1890 and 1917, but by and large labor demands over both economic and political issues were accommodated by the commercial and political elites. In the twentieth century there have been only three periods of significant strife: during World War I, over war-related issues; during the Depression of the 1930s, which inspired protests by workers and the unemployed, eviction riots, and the mobilization in response of a conservative paramilitary group, the New Guard (it took no action); and the late 1960s, when many antiwar demonstrations apparently contributed to the federal government's decision to begin withdrawing troops from Vietnam in 1970.

The Official Records: Public Order Offenses

There are good reasons for expecting that the hostilities evident in civil conflict will also appear in some official indicators of crime. Whereas the vast majority of crimes against persons and property are committed on private account, some are manifestations of collective hostilities and objectives. Individual and group assaults on police and other officials often arise out of political antagonisms. The incidence of such offenses is regularly reported in crime statistics; in some circumstances the offenses so recorded are direct responses to police

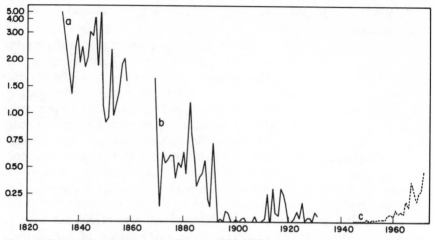

Figure II.2.1 London: Public order offenses, 1834-1972

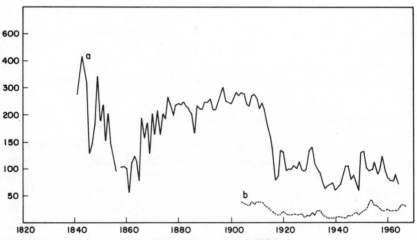

Figure II.2.2 Stockholm: Public order offenses, 1841-1967

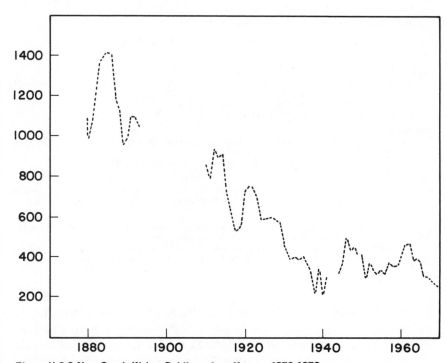

Figure II.2.3 New South Wales: Public order offenses, 1879-1970

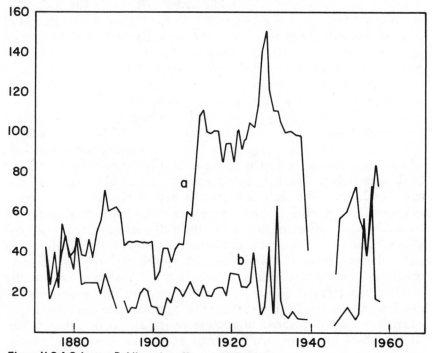

Figure II.2.4 Calcutta: Public order offenses, 1878-1958

Notes to Figures on Public Order Offenses

All figures show annual data weighted per 100,000 population except where noted.

London
 a. Convictions for all indictable cases of assault on the police, riot, treason, unlawful assembly, and similar offenses, Middlesex County, 1834-1858.
 b. Convictions for offenses as in a, MPD, 1869-1931.
 c. Known offenses as in a, MPD, 1945-1972.

Stockholm
 a. Convictions for violence or threats against officials, resistance to officials, and other offenses against public authorities, 1841-1964.
 b. Known offenses of violence or threats against officials, 1904-1967.

New South Wales
 Arrests for assaults on officers and resisting arrest; riot, unlawful assembly, and treason; riotous, offensive, and threatening behavior and language, etc., 1870-1893, 1910-1970.

Calcutta
 a. Convictions for noncognizable offenses against public order per 1,000 population, 1873-1940, 1947-1958. These are minor offenses against a variety of regulatory acts.
 b. Convictions for assaults on public persons, obstruction of justice, group action against authority, and offenses against the state, same years as in a. These are more serious offenses.

efforts to disperse rioters and protestors.[2] Other categories of offense explicitly register the extent of official response to strife and dissent: Some common and obvious examples are arrests and convictions for such offenses as rioting, unlawful assembly, and treason.[3]

The changing incidence of public order offenses in the four cities is indicated in Figures II.2.1 to II.2.4. In each instance we aggregated the offense categories that appeared most likely to reflect acts of political dissent and official repression. Since the graphs give annual rather than averaged data, any correlation with historical episodes of civil strife can be readily seen. The data for London comprise only the more serious (indictable) offenses. They were far more common in the nineteenth than in the twentieth century, and highest of all in the conflict-ridden decades of the 1830s and 1840s. The peak in 1834 may well be a consequence of the Reform Bill demonstrations of the early 1830s; one such occasion in 1833 involved a significant clash with police. Chartist conventions were held in London in 1839 and 1842; only the first corresponds with a blip in the graph. A massive Chartist rally in 1848 coincides with the highest recorded level of public order convictions in the 140-year span. Some but not all peaks in convictions later in the century also can be attributed to particular conflicts. The 1888 peak, for example, follows a bloody encounter between police and socialists in Trafalgar Square the previous November. In the twentieth century the magnitude of convictions is much lower, but the approximate correlation of convictions with episodes of protest continues to be evident. The violent phase of the women's suffrage movement shows up in rising convictions, and so does the tide of antiwar protest of the 1960s.

For Stockholm the data on convictions for public order offenses, line a in Figure II.2.2, include minor as well as serious cases of resistance to police and officials. In the nineteenth and early twentieth centuries it is sometimes possible to associate a peak in offenses with particular events: Major political riots in 1848 and 1864-1865 and the general strike of 1909 are cases in point. But the graph is more informative about the general level of hostility between rulers and citizens. The rising trend that begins in the 1860s coincides with the growth of acute class conflict in Sweden following the limited parliamentary reforms of 1866. That conflict was manifest in a growing number of strikes and protest demonstrations, which subsided after the entrance of the Social Democrats into a ruling coalition in 1917. Universal franchise was introduced between 1918 and 1920; thereafter both measures of public order offenses are much lower and fluctuate irregularly. Increases around 1930 coincide with the increased economic tensions and strike activity of the Depression. In the 1950s substantial strike activity and a number of "issueless riots" seemingly combined to push up the offense rates. The data come to an end shortly after the onset of anti-American protest in the mid-1960s but show no evidence of an upturn. We know from narrative sources that such protest was regarded by Swedish authorities as legitimate, and vestiges of criminal sanctions that might have been applied to it were stricken from the criminal code. In short, the indicators of public order offenses in Stockholm are not surrogate measures of civil strife, but they probably trace the changing intensity of class economic and political tension better than any other available index.

The incidence of arrests for public order offenses in New South Wales (Figure II.2.3.), does not seem to be a valid indicator of strife or of class tensions. During each of three periods of significant strife in the twentieth century—1914-1918, the early 1930s, and the late 1960s—the index is low. The index is comprised largely of arrests for assaults on police and for various offenses in language and behavior. Its 7:1 decline over a period of 85 years speaks plainly about improvements in civility of public behavior and citizen-police interactions in Sydney but is mute about the tensions that underlie civil conflict.

The Calcutta police evidently relied very heavily on regulatory penalties to maintain social control. The upper line in Figure II.2.4 traces the conviction rate per 1,000 for a great variety of offenses against regulations governing public order. Although few of these regulations appear to have had specific political content, they were invoked much more often during periods of civil conflict. The conviction rates are extraordinarily high, too: during the 1920s and 1930s there were rarely less than 100,000 convictions per year, and in years of peak disorder convictions were nearly twice as numerous. In ratio terms, between 1910 and the 1930s the annual conviction rates for these offenses averaged about one for every ten residents of the city. The lower line in the figure traces the conviction rate per 100,000 for a set of uncommon political crimes. Before the turn of the century these rates were relatively high despite the lack of significant civil strife, and convictions for petty public order offenses were relatively low. The inference is that in orderly times criminal sanctions were used to control some kinds of behavior that later were treated as regulatory offenses. In any event both indicators register the principal epochs of twentieth century strife in Calcutta. Both increase beginning in about 1904 and continue upward, irregularly, during two decades of recurring political dissent, communal violence, and the beginning of large-scale strike activity. The peak of police efforts to control opposition apparently came between 1926 and 1934. Among the events of these years were a major communal riot (1926), large-scale political strikes (1928, 1934), and most significant, the Civil Disobedience movement from 1930 to 1934. There was less strife after 1934, and convictions for offenses of both kinds declined accordingly. Data for Calcutta after 1958 indicate that numbers of riots and persons arrested for rioting increased greatly after 1965. These figures are examined in comparison with data on crime later in this chapter.

The principal value of indicators of public order offenses is that they trace rather accurately (except in New South Wales) the extent to which elites use the instrumentalities of the criminal law to maintain political order. Yet these indices should not be expected to mirror exactly the historical episodes of civil strife because open opposition is usually sporadic, whereas official sanctions reflect both elites' ongoing efforts to forestall strife and their intensified efforts to reassert control once open conflict does occur.

Issues, Forms, and Outcomes of Strife:
A Comparative Analysis

Lack of quantified information precludes precise comparisons of magnitudes of civil strife among the cities or within them, but the general patterns emerging from the evidence just summarized are clear enough. Calcutta passed from civil tranquility during the middle years of colonial rule to intense revolutionary resistance and mass agitational politics during the twentieth century. The numbers of people mobilized in these conflict situations, the casualties suffered, and the extent of physical and economic losses sustained far exceed those of the three Western cities in any period we examined. The Western cities are by no means identical in their experience of civil conflict, however. Stockholm experienced episodic conflict through-out the nineteenth century and into the early twentieth century. Such conflict was often deadly in the first half of the nineteenth century, but rarely thereafter. The last 50 years have been largely peaceful ones. Strife in London has been episodic and sometimes pervasive in both centuries but seldom has led to fatalities. Sydney's most turbulent years were in the early twentieth century, from around 1915 to 1935, but the scope and intensity of strife have been so low in the entire history of New South Wales that (aside from clashes with aborigines) we can document no more than a dozen deaths in collective confrontations.

There is, in short, no common long-term trend in magnitudes of civil strife among the cities. Three points of twentieth century similarity in the three Western cities are worth mentioning, however. One is a high level of internal conflict between 1914 and 1918: The combination of war-related issues and preexisting conflicts generated particularly intense economic and political strife in all three cities. This was in marked contrast with the experience of each during World War II. Strike activity remained low during and after that war, and international conflict precipitated few divisive political debates in any of the societies. Last, the international youth "movement" of the 1960s was represented in all three cities. University students and sympathetic members of the middle classes carried out a series of mass protests in which similar tactics were used to oppose groups and policies associated with nuclear armament, the Vietnam war, and apartheid in South Africa. By the middle 1970s such protests had become less frequent and less well attended. They also took on ritualistic qualities evident in an anti-American demonstration held at the United States embassy in Stockholm on July 4, 1975.

Comparisons of the timing and magnitudes of strife may be less instructive than comparisons of parties, issues, tactics, and forms of conflict. Two widely cited generalizations about changing manifesta-tions of conflict in Western societies can be tested against the evidence provided by these cities. One is the observation that "revolutionary" conflict has given way to the politics of reform, compromise, and co-optation.[4] The other, which has been proposed by Charles Tilly, is that collective violence in Western societies has evolved through several stages, from "primitive" communal-based conflict, through reactionary resistance to the demands exacted by expanding national states and economies, to "modern" demands by associational groups for rights and benefits due them.[5]

We have documented the emergence of revolutionary politics in Calcutta in the twentieth century. In the other societies there was very little "revolutionary" conflict even in the nineteenth century, except perhaps in the nightmares of the English elite during the uncertain decades after the French Revolution. Coups in Stockholm were not revolutionary in any contemporary sense; rather, they revealed the existence of factionalism within the elite. Other classes took part in or responded to them only as a function of their affinities for particularly popular or unpopular members of the nobility. London was the site of an isolated incident of revolutionary "putschism" in 1816 in which class interests were at issue, but no class-based support was inspired. In New South Wales a group of disgruntled military officers in 1808 staged a successful coup against Governor William Bligh (who had suffered a similar misadventure at sea a few years previously) because Bligh had tried to stop their trade in smuggled liquor. The principal instance of "revolutionary" activity in twentieth century Sydney was the agitation of a small group of Industrial Workers of the World during the years 1907 to 1916. When Commonwealth legislation declared the IWW to be an unlawful association, 80 of the most active "radicals" presented themselves for arrest. It probably is accurate to say that there has been more *talk* of revolution among intellectuals in the three Western cities in the last decade than at virtually any time in the last two centuries, but not much more action.

Revolutionary activity did not "decline" in these three Western cities, it never was present to a significant degree in the nineteenth or twentieth centuries. The periods we have examined were characterized instead by cycles of group protest and elite resistance to it, followed sooner or later by compromise. There was, moreover, a common thread: Major episodes of protest in these cities usually developed out of the demands of subordinate classes and categories of people for greater political rights and economic benefits. It is tempting to fit such movements into the procrustean bed of economic class analysis. In Stockholm and London the locus of protest shifts over time from the expanding middle class to skilled workers to the new industrial working classes. But the protests of suffragettes, Irish nationalists, and pacifist students cannot readily be described in class terms. The most that can be said is that these diverse groups were all of lower or middle social status, all had distinctive interests and felt that these were being thwarted by the (in)action of powerful others, and all chose tactics of protest, confrontation, and selective violence to advance their interests. It certainly is the case that class-based conflict has declined in Stockholm and Sydney, indeed has all but disappeared as a source of civil strife. Only in strike activity in England is there a substantial element of class hostility. The new issues of protest, especially in the 1960s, have centered not on the distribution of economic benefits or the attainment of political rights but rather on the uses and abuses of political power.

The nature of elite response to protest in the Western societies has had a good deal to do with the issues and forms of urban strife. The immediate response—to demonstrations, riots, and widespread strikes—has rarely been accommodating. Protestors usually have been dispersed, their leaders arrested or harassed, the activists and their organizations subjected to legal and economic sanctions. In longer perspective, though, most of the basic issues of protest have been met by substantial concessions and reforms. Certainly this was true of demands for the extension of the franchise and for the rights of labor to organize and to bargain collectively. All three of the Western societies in the early twentieth century developed powerful labor-based political parties that singly or in coalition have held national power for substantial periods. Viewed individually, the steps by which these changes came about may seem to merit such belittling descriptions as "concession" and "co-optation." Looked at over a 150-year span, however, it is evident that they have been cumulative and little short of revolutionary in their impact: The locus of political power undeniably has moved down the class ladder, and the power of capitalistic enterprises has been sharply constrained by organized labor and prolabor governments, respectively. These separate histories of conflict and accommodation have had two kinds of consequences for civil strife. On the one hand they have preempted revolutionary conflict, by undermining its rationale, incentives, and social bases. On the other, they have created political cultures in which protestors anticipate compromises and elites believe that they are obliged to comply. These mutually reinforcing expectations allow many conflicts to be managed and minimized short of civil strife, and they give a ritualistic quality to incidents that can be called strife.

These generalizations are not necessarily a forecast of civil peace for the indefinite future in these three Western cities or societies. We have pointed out the high level of serious strife in London and have referred to the prevalence of talk of "revolution" among radical intelligentsia. The prevailing methods of conflict management that bind elites and citizens, workers and employers in these societies, are not necessarily applicable to new kinds of issues raised in the last decade or so. Coping with problems of international conflict, persisting inequalities, and alienation and the demand for autonomy in complex societies may be beyond the capacity of elites. In any event such issues may be "nonnegotiable" for growing numbers of the discontented. Indeed, incapacity and intractability may exist side by side. And persisting grievances over irresolvable issues are the seedbed of revolutionary conflict. This is the final objection to generalizations about the conflict-minimizing effects of modernization and urbanization.

The assertion that civil conflict in Western societies has evolved through "stages" characterized by different types of social organization and motives also needs qualification in light of our evidence. The categories themselves can be used for describing most of the civil strife in the three cities. Most strife in all three cities has been what Tilly would call "modern" and has been initiated by associational, class-based groups. Illustrations of his "primitive" category of violence are the various small riots and skirmishes between Anglo-Saxon Londoners and Irish immigrants in the nineteenth century and "coloreds" in the twentieth; the brawls and riots between Stockholmers and soldiers in the nineteenth century might fall into the same group. There are few instances of "reactionary" violence, as Tilly defines the category, but one would not expect to find many in the urban centers of national expansion; these events are more characteristic of people on the periphery. Riotous protests against police actions are one kind of urban example. It also is tempting to use the same classification for the recent protests of alienated youths and intellectuals, because of the presence of a substantial element of reaction to the impersonal and seemingly impervious power of the modern state. There remain instances of civil strife in the cities that do not fit well in any of these three categories. The violent struggles of elite factions for power (limited mainly to early nineteenth-century Stockholm) are one kind of example. Also to be considered are the riotous outbursts of anger and exuberance sprinkled through the histories of all three cities, which have neither explicit rationale nor any target other than the people and property closest to hand. They seem to merit the characterizations of "issueless riots" used by Gary Marx, or "rioting for fun and profit," *pace* Edward Banfield.[6] Such riots were never particularly common in these cities, though, and rarely if ever resulted in the mobilization of the crowds who turned out on the occasion of specific political and economic confrontations.

The assertion that these forms of civil strife evolved in sequence does not seem to be supported by the evidence of these cities over the last 180 years or so. Our judgments are necessarily impressionistic, but protest based on associational groups appears to have been about as common in the early and middle nineteenth century as it has been in the twentieth. Instances of "primitive" violence are as easily found in the twentieth century as in the nineteenth; they have declined markedly in Stockholm, but the same is true of other forms of civil strife. And nothing in history points to the existence of an intervening stage of "reactionary" violence in these three cities. Tilly's generalization is based on data from France, at the national level. Thus we can identify two sources of the discrepancy. The political and social histories of our three societies, especially Sweden and New South Wales, differ markedly from the case of France and give us little reason to expect civil strife to have similar social forms and bases in the same historical sequence. Equally important, we would expect strife in dominant cities to have different characteristics from strife occurring elsewhere. We suggest, on the basis of limited evidence, that with great historical consistency civil strife in the Western cities has arisen mainly from the demands of "associational" economic groups and political factions. The generalization applies with some certainty to London, Stockholm, and Sydney during the past 180 years.

There is little point in testing generalizations about civil strife in Western cities against the experience of a non-Western city like Calcutta because no one has claimed those generalizations to be relevant. In Calcutta civil strife evolved from protest to rebellion and revolution, under conditions that are familiar from a general theoretical perspective: Each successive round of Bengali nationalist agitation was met by coercive response of sufficient severity to bring it to a gradual halt. In the ensuing periods of relative tranquility the suppressive measures were gradually relaxed. Since few substantial concessions or adjustments were made by the colonial elite during the lulls, nationalist agitation reemerged more or less quickly, usually with more adamant and less negotiable demands. These cycles continued until the British capitulated, having lost the will and means to resist further. The general principle is that the mix of inconsistent repression and lack of reform is usually fatal to the elites who employ it.[7] Another generalization can be drawn by contrasting the political cultures that have evolved in the four cities, with special reference to conflict and conciliation. Certain patterns of mutual expectations of compromise have evolved among most groups in the three Western cities and societies, in sharp contrast to the readiness of contending groups in Calcutta to use mass agitation and violence in all conflict situations. The difference need not be attributed to some vague "cultural difference" between Eastern and Western or "modern" and "underdeveloped" societies. It is more simply explained by the very different historical experiences of these societies: In three of them traditions of gradual elite accommodation emerged, whereas in the fourth victory has gone to the groups whose reliance on force has been most persistent and uncompromising.

The last issue addressed here is whether there is anything distinctively "urban" about the patterns of civil strife we have traced. A number of features evidently are dependent on the urban setting. The prevalence of associational groups in conflict, even in Calcutta, is a function of urban occupational and mobility patterns, which cut across and erode the primary ties that bind communal groups together. Moreover, a "critical mass" of disaffected citizenry is more often to be found in cities than elsewhere, which means also that cities are promising places to organize agitational politics. This relationship holds true regardless of whether there is proportionally more disaffection among city dwellers than among their counterparts in the towns and country: People are more readily organized in the cities. By the same token, people also are more easily observed and policed in the cities than the country. In the face of modern armies and police forces, dissidents who initiate conflict in urban areas are likely to select less violent and provocative tactics, and they are unlikely to be able to carry out sustained "revolutionary" action. A fourth distinctive property of urban settings, especially metropolises such as those we studied, is that the agents who are responsible for grievances, or capable of resolving them, are more likely to be found there. Thus targeted protest accompanied by carefully formulated demands is more likely to occur in cities, too. In addition to these generalizations it is evident that the concerns and grievances of city people usually differ from those of the rural element. The former are less concerned with land than with jobs, less with separatism or resistance to government agents than with sharing or seizing power. It is tempting to use these generalizations as a basis for proposing that many of the typical characteristics of civil strife in "modern" societies—limited demands, associational base, high degree of organization, relatively nonviolent and nonrevolutionary character—are partly a function of their urban setting. The evidence examined here is only suggestive; it provides no test of the assertion.

CRISES OF PUBLIC ORDER: THE COINCIDENCE OF CONFLICT AND CRIME

We have documented the trends in individual crime and the episodic nature of civil strife in four societies. The next question is one we posed earlier. Does any correlation exist between the outbreak of civil conflict and short-term increases in common crime? Our use of the portmanteau concept "public disorder" presumes some correspondence between the two faces of disorder. In later chapters we review evidence that both conditions have often stimulated similar kinds of official response, especially the expansion and reform of police forces. Calcutta has furnished suggestive evidence on the point: Almost all indicators of crime rose sharply at about the time of the onset of nationalist agitation.

There are at least three reasons for expecting to find a general relationship between high crime and civil conflict. One of the most pervasive assumptions of theories of crime and conflict is that both are rooted in social tensions that are manifest in a prevailing sense of individual anomie, alienation, or discontent. It is plausible to suppose that such states of mind will motivate some to join in collective action and others, depending on their needs and opportunities, to take more individualistic courses of action. A second line of argument is that widespread and prolonged group conflict causes or increases the breakdown of moral order. People in disorderly times are more likely to do what they feel like doing than what others say is right and proper. A third factor is that elites faced with real or threatened resistance probably intensify efforts at social control across the board, increasing policing, prosecuting, and punishment. The changing incidence of public order offenses, reviewed earlier, offers one proof of this connection. The additional evidence summarized below neither tests nor assumes the accuracy of any one of these arguments. Together, though, they give us more than sufficient reason for expecting a positive but less than perfect connection between conflict and crime.

The first step in testing the crime-conflict nexus was to identify systematically what are popularly called "crime waves." We decided to include each period in which the crime rate increased in three successive years at an average rate of ten percent a year or more. The procedure was applied separately to indicators of violent crime and theft for each of the four societies. Four to eight "waves" of increases in each type of crime were identified in each city, most of them three to four years in duration, a few lasting ten years or more. Then the extent of strife in each period of rising crime was assessed, based on the narrative accounts reviewed earlier in this chapter. Whenever two or all three kinds of disorder increased simultaneously, we label them a "crisis of public order." The results are summarized in Tables II.2.1 to II.2.4, which we discuss separately, then comparatively.[8]

In 150 years of London's history there were seven instances of sharp increases in crimes of violence and eight in theft (Table II.2.1). A number of these periods coincided approximately or precisely with serious conflict, constituting six distinct crises of public order. Their approximate dates are 1830-1832, 1842-1848, 1874-1882, 1916-1920, 1925-1931, and 1956-1972. With the exception of 1874-1882, which corresponds with a sharp economic decline, all are marked by increasing crime and strife. Both theft and violent crimes usually increased during one of these episodes (1830-1832 is the single exception), lending added force to the argument that the two facets of disorder are closely interconnected. The relationship is by no means perfect, however. There are four periods of sharply rising crime rates (one in the 1820s, three between 1890 and 1907) during which no significant strife occurred. And the five years before the outbreak of World War I—a time of intense political protest in London, especially by the suffragettes—had no noticeable effect on the rate of common crime.

Table II.2.1 Crises of Public Order in London, 1820-1972

Years of rising crime rates[a]	Average increase in violent crime (%)[b]	Average increase in theft (%)[c]	Evidence of civil strife
1825-1827		24	None in London; economic riots elsewhere, 1826-1827
1830-1832	49		Agitation for Reform Bill of 1832; widespread riots and strikes throughout England
1842-1845	13	14	Major Chartist demonstrations in London, 1842 and 1848, in context of national workers' movement 1838-1848
1845-1848	16	11	
1874-1876		10	No significant strife; 1875-1880 was a period of sharp economic decline
1877-1882		17	
1891-1899			No significant strife
1901-1903			No significant strife
1905-1907	14		No significant strife
1916-1920		26	Widespread strikes, 1919-1921
1918-1920	37		
1925-1928	16	26	General strike of 1926; significant strike activity 1929-1932
1928-1931			
1956-1972	12	12	Large-scale political protest over various issues; small-scale ethnic clashes; substantial strike activity 1957, 1969-1971

a. Periods in which crime rates increased for at least three consecutive years at an average rate of at least 10 percent per year.
b. Average annual percentage increases for indictable offenses of murder and assault, convictions before 1920, known offenses thereafter.
c. Average annual percentage increases for indictable theft, convictions before 1920, known offenses thereafter.

Table II.2.2 Crises of Public Order in Stockholm, 1840-1971

Years of rising crime rates[a]	Average increase in violent crime (%)[b]	Average increase in theft (%)[c]	Evidence of civil strife
1850-1852		11	No significant strife
1866-1868		26	No significant strife
1874-1876	24		Serious clashes with police and soldiers, three in 1875 alone
1880-1876		12	Substantial labor protest, continued clashes with police. In the decade five riots, twelve demonstrations, and numerous strikes were recorded
1881-1890	83		
1899-1905	49		High level of strike activity; serious clashes between police and strikers in 1900 and 1905
1916-1918		43	The "hunger years"; many demonstrations and a food riot
1938-1942		25	No significant strife
1938-1945	46		Minor street clashes
1947-1949		14	
1952-1958	26		Minor street clashes, significant strike activity
1961-1963	26		
1963-1970		10	Numerous antiforeign protests, few strikes or clashes
1965-1967	28		

a. Periods in which crime rates increased for at least three consecutive years at an average rate of at least 10 percent per year.
b. Average of annual percentage increases for known offenses of murder and attempts. The percentages are high because such offenses are few in number and subject to great annual variation.
c. Average annual percentage increases for all known offenses of theft, including burglary, robbery, larceny, and auto theft. Figures before 1870 based on conviction data.

In Stockholm fifteen epochs of rising reported crime also qualify as "crime waves," across a span of 130 years (Table II.2.2), and ten of them were associated with significant strife. We have already referred several times to class tensions in Sweden during the latter decades of the nineteenth century and the early years of the twentieth. Stockholm's crises of public order of 1874-1876, 1880-1890, and 1899-1905 are related to these tensions. The next crisis, in 1916-1918, was directly a consequence of economic collapse, for the economy of neutral Sweden suffered even more in World War I than in the next war, which was also accompanied by rising crime rates. In the years after 1945 there are three identifiable surges in crime rates, the last two coinciding with significant strife. The distinctions among them may be arbitrary, for the trend in crime rates has been up since 1947. The onset of strife came well after the rise in crime, however, and touched on seemingly unrelated economic and political issues. When we turn the situation around and identify major periods of conflict that were not accompanied by rising crime rates, we find two: the struggle of the middle class for greater political rights, which lasted into the 1840s (there were devastating riots of 1848), and the strike-ridden years of the 1920s and early 1930s (just under half of the 685 strikes recorded in Stockholm between 1900 and 1970 occurred in these two decades).

New South Wales provides another set of tests (Table II.2.3). Between 1830 and 1970 there were nine marked increases in conviction rates for violent crime and five for theft. We already have remarked on the low level of civil conflict in New South Wales during most of its history, and it is not surprising that six of these fourteen "crime waves" occurred independently of strife. It is perhaps more surprising that eight of the fourteen do coincide with strife. The first episodes of large-scale working-class protest, in 1886-1888, coincide precisely with a rise in convictions for both kinds of common crime, and a similar pattern is repeated in 1918-1923. The effects of the Depression also are evident in the form of a simultaneous rise in economic crime and economic protest. When the relationship is examined from the perspective of strife, we find that there are eight five-year periods of detectable strife between 1850 and 1970, and only one—economic protest in the early 1860s—is not matched by rising crime. On the whole, the correlation between rising crime and civil conflict in New South Wales is as strong as it is in the two European cities.

The evidence from Calcutta on this issue is mixed. In the span of 99 years for which we have convictions data (Table II.2.4) there is evidence for six distinct crises of public order: 1876-1879, 1906-1910, 1918-1920, 1923-1926, 1931-1933, and 1956-1959. Convictions for crime and strife rise simultaneously in all but the

Table II.2.3 Crises of Public Order in New South Wales, 1830-1970

Years of rising crime rates[a]	Average increase in violent crime (%)[b]	Average increase in theft (%)[c]	Evidence of civil strife
1853-1855	27		No significant strife
1871-1873	33		No significant strife
1886-1888[d]	32	28	First large-scale labor protests and strikes, 1885-1888
1898-1900	21		Minor apolitical street clashes
1907-1914	37		Significant strike activity, 1907 and after
1918-1923	19	14	Major strikes in 1917, 1919, some postwar street fighting
1929-1931[d]		15	Major strikes in 1929; recurrent demonstrations, eviction riots, street fighting in early 1930s
1937-1939		19	No significant strife
1940-1942	30		No significant strife
1946-1950	11		Significant strike activity, small-scale protests
1954-1961		10	No significant strife
1967-1969	19		Many antiwar and antiapartheid demonstrations

a. Periods in which crime rates increased for at least three consecutive years at an average annual rate of at least 10 percent. There were no periods of substantial increase between 1830 and 1852.
b. Average of annual percentage in higher court convictions for murder and assault.
c. Average of annual percentage increases in higher court convictions for theft.
d. Period includes two years of very substantial increase and one year of slight decline.

first of these six instances. Three crises coincide with three of the four principal nationalist campaigns, and crime data are lacking for the fourth one, the Quit India movement of 1942-1943. Most of the major episodes of communal violence in the city's history also coincide with short-term increases in crime. The exceptions are posed by strike activity. Widespread political and economic strikes in 1921, 1928, 1934, and 1953-1954 are not matched by rising rates of violent crime or theft.

An examination of more detailed evidence for the 1960s, though, shows relations among strife, crime, and official behavior that are different and more complex. Some of the relevant data are set out in Figure II.2.5; since the time span is short and population estimates are unreliable, the data are not weighted by population. It is strikingly evident that during these years the recorded levels of crime and official efforts at control were greatest when strife was low. From 1963 through 1966 more than 20,000 cognizable (serious) offenses were recorded per year, and officials were able to obtain convictions for more than two-thirds of them. (For India's eight largest cities in 1965, by contrast, the average conviction rate for cognizable offenses known was 41 percent.) The most serious offenses—murder, armed robbery, and dacoity—numbered less than 100 per year during this period, and "riots" (collective disturbances by five or more individuals) were at a relatively low level of 200 to 300 per year.

Beginning in 1966 riots and arrests for rioting began a five-year increase of 400 percent, paralleled by a sevenfold increase in the most serious individual crimes. These are the official tracings of a crisis of public order of the most serious magnitude, precipitated mainly by the Communist Party of India (CPI), which in 1966 organized a massive series of food agitations, strikes, and violent demonstrations aimed at toppling the Congress Party Government of Bengal. After the 1967 elections the CPI joined the new left-wing United Front Government, whose effects on public order are evident in the official statistics. By 1971 (following a period of direct rule by the central government) the total number of serious offenses known to police had dropped by more than half, arrests and trials declined by ratios of 5:1 or more, and convictions were obtained for scarcely 20 percent of what was now a much smaller number of "known" cases. The phenomenon was peculiar to Calcutta. In India's other large cities there were no comparable declines in known offenses, and in 1971 convictions were obtained in an average of 44 percent of all known cases.[9]

The impact of civil strife associated with the rise and fall of the United Front Government on crime and the criminal justice system in Calcutta was very great. Evidently a concerted effort was made to improve public order in the city under the Congress Party regime in

Table II.2.4 Crises of Public Order in Calcutta, 1873-1971

Years of rising crime rates[a]	Average increase in violent crime (%)[b]	Average increase in theft (%)[c]	Evidence of civil strife
1876-1879	48	15	No significant strife
1906-1908	15	13	Antipartition movement, first overt nationalist strife, 1906-1908
1906-1910			
1918-1920	26	14	First major communal riots 1918, otherwise a quiet period characterized by economic recession
1923-1926	15		Last phase of noncooperation movement, 1920-1924; major communal rioting, 1926
1931-1933	13		Civil disobedience movement, 1930-1934
1957-1958		44	Major economic and political strikes 1954-1957 but not in 1958 or 1959
1956-1959	107		

a. Periods in which crime rates increased for at least three consecutive years (except 1957-1958) at an average annual rate of at least 10 percent.

b. Average of annual percentage increases in convictions for murder and assault.

c. Average of annual percentage increases in convictions for noncognizable (minor) theft.

the early and mid-1960s. During that time the police and courts were very assiduous in detecting offenses, arresting suspects, and securing convictions. Because of altered political circumstances thereafter, the institutions of public order suspended most of their routine control activities and, apparently, did little more than record and react to the rising incidence of rioting, murder, and robbery.

The immediate conclusion to be drawn from these comparisons is that sharp increases in indicators of crimes of violence and theft usually coincide with episodes of strife. Objective criteria have been used to identify 29 substantial increases in violent crime, measured mostly by reference to changes in conviction rates. Nineteen of the 29, or 66 percent, coincided with serious internal conflict. Of the increases in theft, thirteen of 25 also coincided with civil strife. Since neither "crime waves" nor episodes of strife are particularly common in these cities (except for strife in Calcutta), there is not much doubt that the correlation reflects the existence of a pervasive and important social phenomenon. The simplest explanation—that periods of strife provide greater opportunities for crime—is probably insufficient. When social tension is widespread and intense, it is likely to provoke different forms of disorder at the same time that it spurs elites and officials to intensified efforts at control. In extreme cases disorder rises to such a pitch that the authorities are reduced to impotence. Two examples of this occurred in Calcutta, in the mid-1940s and in the late 1960s.

This study does not specify the more remote social causes of crime and strife, which would be necessary to test this kind of hypothesis. The three chapters that follow are concerned instead with how the law, police, and judicial institutions have defined, reported, and responded to the diverse conditions of public order. As institutions have changed, so has public disorder, exhibiting a recurring pattern of interdependence that is as enduring as it is antagonistic.

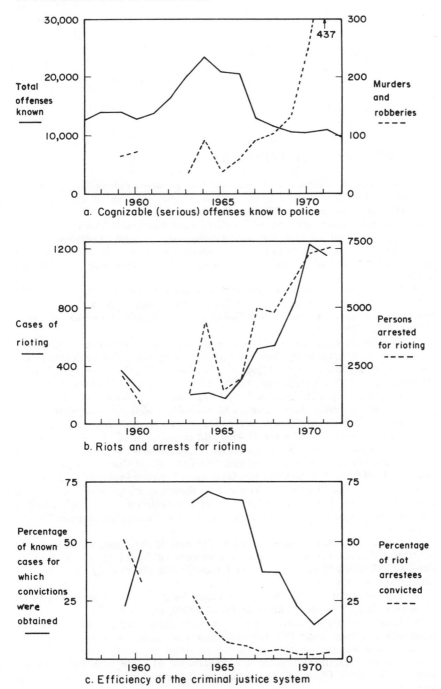

Figure II.2.5 Calcutta: Indicators of crime, conflict, and the administration of justice, 1957-1972

NOTES TO PART II, CHAPTER 2

1. See Peter N. Grabosky, "Protest and the Quiescent Polity: Public Order in Sydney, 1788-1973," paper given at the Annual Meeting of the American Political Science Association, Chicago, September 1974.

2. Not all rioters act out of political conviction, and many attacks on policemen are motivated by the common impulse to resist or retaliate against arrest. Unlike the other crimes we have examined, however, a significant proportion of the offenses so categorized are likely to have diffuse or specific political content.

3. In a study of "protest" crimes in nineteenth-century England, George Rudé so categorizes arson, riot, machine-breaking, high treason, sedition, and breach of the peace, in "Protest and Punishment in Nineteenth Century Britain," *Albion*, 5 (1973), 1-23.

4. The debate over the "end of ideology" includes as one of its elements the subsidence of revolutionary demands and tactics by the urban proletariat. See, for example, Seymour Martin Lipset, *Political Man: The Social Bases of Politics* (Garden City, N.Y.: Doubleday, 1960), chs. 2, 3, and 7; Mostafa Rejai, ed., *Decline of Ideology* (Chicago: Aldine, 1971), and C. I. Waxman, *The End of Ideology Debate* (New York: Funk and Wagnalls, 1969). Contemporary cross-national comparisons of the characteristics of civil conflict document the high frequency and intensity of internal wars and conspiracies in non-Western countries by comparison with Western countries, from which historical trends away from revolution are sometimes inferred. See Ted Robert Gurr, "A Comparative Study of Civil Strife," in Graham and Gurr, eds., *Violence in America*, ch. 17.

5. Charles Tilly, "Collective Violence in European Perspective," in Graham and Gurr, eds., ch. 1, and "The Changing Place of Collective Violence" in Melvin Richter, ed., *Essays in Social and Political History* (Cambridge: Harvard University Press, 1970).

6. See Gary T. Marx, "Issueless Riots," *Annals of the American Academy of Political and Social Science*, vol. 391 (September 1970), 21-33, and Edward C. Banfield, "Rioting Mainly for Fun and Profit," *The Unheavenly City* (Boston: Little, Brown, 1970), ch. 9.

7. The argument is made and various examples cited in Gurr, *Why Men Rebel* (Princeton, N.J.: Princeton University Press, 1970), esp. ch. 8.

8. More precise comparisons require more complete and precise data on the incidence and magnitude of strife than could be gathered in this study. The principal disadvantage of the procedure followed is not imprecision but its failure to test systematically for the occurrence of strife without correlated increases in crime. Observations on this point are included in the subsequent discussion.

9. The data on Calcutta and other Indian cities during this period are from annual editions of *Crime in India* (New Delhi: Ministry of Home Affairs).

Chapter 3

ELITE INTERESTS AND THE
DEFINITION OF PUBLIC ORDER

The nature of elites' concerns about public disorder is most concretely revealed in the institutions they establish and the policies they follow in the ongoing effort to manage conflict and control crime. The next three chapters compare the evolution of institutions and policies in four societies, with particular reference to the nature and scope of criminal law, the development of police forces, and the judicial and penal treatment accorded offenders. Of special interest are the timing and circumstances of changes in these institutions, and the ways in which such changes appear to have affected the extent and severity of public disorder.

Most of the discussion is concerned with national or colonywide policies and institutions rather than with those of the four cities alone. With some exceptions, however, the policies and institutions we examine were devised in response to metropolitan interests and problems and were implemented at least as quickly and thoroughly in primary cities as elsewhere. Therefore a "national" analysis is fully and often especially applicable to the cities.

ELITE INTERESTS

We begin with a consideration of the kinds of values and objectives that elites apply to questions of public order. The "elites" of concern are the groups and individuals—mainly political leaders and officials, but also the spokesmen for powerful economic and social groups— who make the fundamental decisions about public order policies. By focusing on elites we are not assuming that their interests and values are necessarily different from or antithetical to those of other social strata. As far as we can tell, the elites of all the societies examined here have shared some values and norms with other major social groups—even in Bengal during colonial rule. The differences are variable over time and become apparent both in the patterns of strife and crime and in public demands for changes in law and policy. Those demands sometimes have substantial effects, and this reveals another aspect of our conception of the role of elites in defining and policing public order: They are not autonomous but rather are subject to various kinds of influences and constraints. The values and social beliefs held by elites in common with other members of society are one latent kind of constraint. The bureaucratic inertia of established police, judicial, and penal systems is another. It is evident, especially in contemporary societies, that many well-intentioned elite attempts to alter, say, police and penal policies, are thwarted by the passive resistance or incapacity of lower echelon members of those institutions. External pressures for change, on the other hand, come from a variety of sources: sometimes from the general public, concerned about crime or pernicious policy, sometimes from special interest groups, sometimes from the intellectuals and experts who mold opinion, elite as well as public. Thus it is too simplistic to maintain that changing policies of public order are merely manifestations of an elite's class interests or narrow desire to retain power. Class and conservative interests are often evident in public order policies, but so are many other conditions.

The following summary of the most salient elite concerns about public order in the four societies makes reference to two major dimensions of variation: first the extent to which issues of public order have been of primary concern to elites, and second, the extent to which elite interests in defining and policing public order appear to have diverged from the concerns of other social groups.

Public order issues were of the greatest salience for the British who ruled Bengal. The achievement of British economic ends in Bengal depended in the most fundamental way on eliminating or at least controlling organized Indian resistance to British rule. Individual crime was of less concern, except insofar as it affected the British population and their clients and employees. The control of crime among Indians was a low-priority item during most of the colonial period, as is evident from the scanty resources devoted to the relevant institutions of public order, as well as from the retrenchment of ordinary crime prevention activities during periods of heightened nationalist activity. Circumstances have not changed greatly since independence. The persistence of revolutionary opposition to the new Indian rulers of West Bengal and the enduring tradition of mass agitational politics in Calcutta pose a real and continuing threat to both political and economic elites. The city's economic decline has increased the need and reduced the resources for public services of all kinds. It is not surprising, given these conditions, that the control of common crime receives fewer resources and more perfunctory attention than in Western societies.

The rulers of (West) Bengal have had relatively little to fear from individual Indians compared with the uneasiness caused the authorities of New South Wales by convicts during the first half-century of the colony. The maintenance of order among a population comprised substantially of transported convicts and Irish nationalists was a paramount end in itself in the early years. The necessity for tight and punitive control was reinforced by the prevailing British belief in the inherent depravity of the "criminal class." In the early nineteenth century the development of labor-intensive agriculture, employing convict and ex-convict labor, furnished an explicitly economic incentive for maintaining, even tightening coercive control. By midcentury, however, public order was no longer a dominant issue, thanks to three factors: the end of transportation in 1840, the upsurge in the number of voluntary immigrants, and the rising agricultural prosperity of a colony that "rode the sheep's back" through the rest of the century. It probably is accurate to say that for the past century and more, the principal concerns of the New South Wales and Commonwealth elites have been continued economic prosperity and the provision of public and social services, with the relative emphasis varying according to whether working-class or middle-class parties were in power. Public order has become a salient issue only when disorder seemed to threaten the economic system or middle-class conceptions of proper social and sexual conduct.

The threat of crime and revolution weighed very heavily on the English elite from the end of the Napoleonic wars well into the 1840s. Beginning late in the eighteenth century, Britain, like most other European societies, suffered from the first phase of the population "explosion" that has continued to the present. For several decades the consequence was a labor surplus and the progressive immiseration of the urban and rural lower classes. By contemporary standards—and, what is more important, by the standards of the previous century—the poor were "overworked, atrociously housed, undernourished, disease-ridden and lived in a misery that defies the modern imagination."[1] Many were forced into beggary and petty thievery to exist at all, and a few were both desperate and well-nourished enough to cherish hopes of revolution. The English elite's fears of revolution proved to be illusory, partly because of the expanding economic opportunities that accompanied the "take-off" of the Industrial Revolution. The problems of crime were more obvious and pervasive, but they too proved tractable. This period of crisis coincided with what Asa Briggs has called "the age of improvement," during which most of the leaders of English society became supremely confident of their capacity to create a moral, industrious, prosperous—hence orderly—society. The conditions that bred the "criminal class" and crime were thought to be remediable, along with other social ills, and the developments of the Victorian era, during which public order improved dramatically, seemed to justify a positive attitude.[2]

In some contrast to this early optimism is the mixture of toleration and resignation with which most members of English society seem to regard rising disorder in recent decades. Officials, journalists, and ordinary citizens are concerned, some of them intensely, but there are at least two noteworthy characteristics of elite and popular attitudes toward crime and strife in English society. The fear, hysteria, and advocacy of draconian measures that typify the North American reaction to the problem have been rare in England for over a century. Even the political bombings in the 1970s have evoked responses much more defensive than repressive. Second, there are no major episodes of public moralism in our study of London comparable to those we observed in Sydney (of which more later). That is, whereas the New South Welshmen have often made intense but short-lived elite, legislative, police, and judicial efforts to control particular kinds of offenses—usually having to do with sex, drugs, or public behavior—the tides of English concern have risen and fallen more gently. Our conclusion is that since the 1850s public order in English society generally, and in London in particular, has rarely been any more than a secondary concern for most of the elite or the public at large. The principal exception to this generalization came during the years immediately before World War I, as discussed in the next chapter.

Several themes are evident in the history of elite concern about public order in Stockholm. The rise of liberal middle-class dissent in the first half of the nineteenth century was perceived as a threat calling for legal and judicial response by the monarchy and the nobility. In the last two decades of the nineteenth century and the first years of the twentieth, the economic and political demands of the working class stimulated substantial efforts at controlling strikes and other kinds of protest. In the aftermath of the Russian Revolution there was considerable concern about revolutionary prospects in Sweden, and these fears may have contributed to the decision to grant universal suffrage in 1921. A second, recurring issue has been public behavior, drunkenness and vagrancy in particular. Both economic and social motives were evident in official efforts to control such activities: Vagrancy, mainly a nineteenth century problem, was usually synonymous with unemployment; the personal and social costs of alcoholism have attracted the concerted efforts of reformers representing various strata of Swedish society for well over a century. Notably absent is apparent, intense concern by the Swedish elite about "ordinary" crimes of violence or theft. The marked differences over time in the reported incidence of these crimes have not inspired comparable official efforts at control. To the elite, they seem to have appeared less threatening then either civil strife or disorderly individual behavior.

Thus far we have assessed the salience of civil strife and crime for the elites in these four societies, making only passing reference to the views of non-elites. The interests of the latter have been very diverse and mostly undocumented, and our conclusions and comparisons on this issue are more tentative. We suggest, first, that dissent and civil strife have been the subjects of the greatest divergence of opinion in all the societies. The reasons are obvious: Most political and economic strife in the societies has had a class basis and the objective of curtailing some of the powers and privileges of the dominant classes. In the three Western societies there has also been a gradual convergence of interest between rulers and ruled on the issue of strife and dissent. One does not have to accept the "end of ideology" thesis to recognize that there has been a significant increase in the political and economic power wielded by working-class organizations. The old upper classes have largely dissolved, and the old and new middle and professional classes are generally acquiescent about power-sharing. As a consequence the social basis for strife has lessened, and something like consensus exists on the need for cooperation and conflict management. These assertions are most applicable to Sweden and New South Wales, they need some qualification with reference to Britain, where important segments of the labor movement intransigently hold to revolutionary objectives (if nationalization can still be said to be "revolutionary") and disruptive means to that end. Radical student and intellectual protest in England and in Australian society is also outside the consensual pale, not necessarily in its objectives but certainly in its reliance on tactics of civil disobedience. Strife of this kind has only a small social base and is rejected by most other social groups. The foregoing generalizations do not apply in West Bengal, where elite and popular opinion remain acrimoniously at odds over what public order ought to be and which groups should define and maintain it.

The realm of social behavior and morality continues to divide social opinion in the three Western societies. One distinctive consequence of the growing influence of the middle classes in the nineteenth century was their attempt to impose their standards of behavior on other social classes. The list of behaviors that have been the subject of recurrent attempts at regulation is highly similar across all three societies. It is also long and sometimes ludicrous, and

includes idleness, lack of regular employment, infidelity, homosexuality, abortion, prostitution, public urination and profanity,
gambling, alcohol consumption, the private distilling of alcohol, and
the use of drugs other than alcohol. The first few items on this list
now largely escape attempts at official regulation; most of the others
are the subject of sporadic or persistent, and often strenuous, efforts
at control. What is at issue, of course, is the conflict between the
desires of people with the least stake in society to "do what feels
good" and the desire of those who have more stake, and are armed
with moral tenets of religious origin, to limit what they perceive as
the socially corrosive effects of indulgence. The nineteenth century
Victorians were remarkably successful in persuading most of the
working class of the rightness of their views on these issues, and we
infer from limited evidence that middle-class values on most of these
matters became pervasive in Swedish and Australian society too.
Coincident with World War I, however, some well-documented
changes began to occur in middle-class notions of morality and
deviance, followed by modifications in demands for public order and
the definition of it. To simplify grossly what has happened in the
past 50 years, attempts to regulate sexual conduct have largely
ceased in London and Stockholm (though not in New South Wales);
drug use is of intense concern in Stockholm and Sydney; while
public drunkenness is both common and rather consistently policed
in all three Western cities. Sydney appears to be the most "moralistic" of the three in the Victorian sense, London is distinctly the
least. Both Sydney and Stockholm seem to be characterized now by
consensus across classes about such issues, though there are definite
differences between the cities. English opinion seems to be more
sharply divided, with the professional and intellectual classes leading
the libertarian way over the resistance of much of the lower middle
and skilled working classes.

In Bengal the British imported their version of social morality
beginning in the eighteenth century and in some instances attempted
to apply their standards not only to the foreign community but to
Indians as well. The British were particularly offended by the Indian's use of infanticide as a form of birth control and did what they
could to discourage the practice. It seems to have been resorted to
more in rural than in urban areas, and rarer than contemporary
accounts imply. Another offensive practice was suttee, the immola-
tion of widows with the bodies of their husbands. In the early
nineteenth century there were several hundred instances each year in
Calcutta. The major impetus for outlawing the custom did not come
from the British, though, but from Bengali Hindus who found the
practice morally objectionable. For the most part one receives the

impression that "deviance" among Indians went unpoliced or was left to indigenous courts and traditional patterns of control. British attempts to ensure the humane treatment of animals in the city, for example, were given up for want of police resources. We have no direct evidence about contemporary Bengali opinion on these matters, but the rates of arrests and convictions for offenses of the types just listed are very low or nonexistent. Offenses against standards of social conduct are not necessarily rare in Bengal society, but they seem to be under informal social control much more than in Western societies.

The kinds of crime about which social consensus is probably greatest in all four societies are murder, assault, and the various forms of acquisitive crime. In Part I we observed that there is some social relativity in what constitutes theft or crimes against the person, but these kinds of offenses are what most people have in mind when they excoriate crime. We have no evidence of substantial disagreement across classes in the four cities about the undesirability of these behaviors, with two kinds of exceptions. Some small revolutionary groups in twentieth century Calcutta and London have justified certain kinds of murder and theft as political tactics. It also could be argued that high rates of theft are prima facie evidence that some groups, otherwise voiceless, value stealing other people's property. Yet it is safe to say that these groups have not been tolerant about assault and theft when they are the victims. The social differences of opinion about murder, theft, and assault in the Western cities (we lack evidence for Calcutta) have centered not on whether these behaviors are social evils, but rather on how to deal with them.

We conclude this commentary on elite and popular interests in public order by pointing out that recent increases in public disorder in the Western cities have been most pronounced in offenses that are both commonly abhorred and widely felt. The agreement of ordinary citizens, police, judges, and elites on the reality of ascending statistics on assault and theft is further evidence of the behavioral as well as social truth of this phenomenon. But there is something paradoxical about public response to the issue. One would expect this kind of commonly perceived problem to stimulate concerted public demands and programmatic official response. In fact the elite and governmental response has been relatively tolerant. At least two plausible explanations come to mind. One is paralyzing lack of agreement among interested parties about the most effective policies to follow. Second, elites and officials are in fact relatively little concerned about these kinds of crime because their costs—unlike the costs of civil strife—are sustained mainly by ordinary citizens, who are most likely to be assaulted and who bear, directly and indirectly, most of the costs of personal and commercial theft.

THE EVOLUTION OF CRIMINAL CODES

Criminal law establishes the framework within which policies of public order are carried out. Much of the criminal law on the books at any one time is only selectively applied or has been allowed to lapse into disuse. But changes and reforms in criminal codes reflect the evolution of elite and public attitudes toward public order. In Western societies, and others that have accepted the Western legal tradition, changes in law are telling manifestations of shifting goals and values of the elite, and of changing patterns of group influence on policies of public order. Even if legal changes are made for the sake of show rather than action (a motive we think has been relatively uncommon in the four societies during the era we studied), they reveal much about the values and social interests to which decision makers believe they must be symbolically responsive.

The criminal laws of all four societies have been recurrently revised and modernized during the last 200 years. This is the chronological skeleton. English criminal law at the beginning of the nineteenth century consisted of a core of uncodified common law overlaid by a hodgepodge accumulation of acts of Parliament prescribing criminal penalties for a great many specific activities—e.g., stealing from bleaching-grounds, appearing armed and disguised, consorting with gypsies, and participation in a combination of workers seeking increases in wages. All but the last were punishable by death; as of 1820 so were at least 200 other offenses, minor as well as serious. This reliance on the death penalty was a fixture of seventeenth and especially eighteenth century political thought and criminal law throughout Europe: Capital punishment was widely regarded as the most effective deterrent to crime. English juries and judges often were reluctant to convict because they thought the death penalty too severe in specific cases, and throughout the eighteenth century a great many sentences of death were commuted to transportation, the second pillar of English penal practice at the time.[3] Attempts at reform early in the nineteenth century culminated in a series of acts in the late 1820s and 1830s that consolidated and simplified criminal law. The number of capital offenses was greatly reduced during the same period, and transportation to all penal colonies was finally ended in 1867. A set of acts passed in 1861 effected a further consolidation and ended capital punishment for crimes other than murder and treason. Throughout the nineteenth and twentieth centuries many specific acts have modified aspects of the criminal law, but there have been no eras of change comparable in scope to those just cited. Two liberalizing changes in the 1960s worth special mention were the abolition of capital punishment and the decriminalization of homosexuality between consenting adults. There was also, in 1968, a general consolidation of statutes applying to the various kinds of theft.

The criminal law of New South Wales derived from English common law also, but a great many acts have been added. Only two wholesale revisions have been made, in 1883 and 1900, and neither constituted a comprehensive criminal code. The act of 1900 was modified by no less than 37 amending acts through 1972, though most of the modifications have been procedural not substantive. The severity of sentences prescribed has declined markedly, as in Britain. Capital and corporal punishments were less often specified in law and much less often applied after the end of transportation in 1840. It was not until 1955, however, that capital punishment was formally abolished (for all offenses except treason and piracy), and whipping remained a legally permissible penalty until 1974. Virtually all the enactments of criminal law in New South Wales during the last 75 years remain on the books; there has been almost no formal decriminalization. The only substantial exception was the establishment of state-run off-track betting in 1965, which in effect legalized a durable and popular pastime that the police had never effectively controlled.

Bengal was governed by the East India Company through 1858, and its patchwork of European and "native" courts applied both English and Indian law, depending on the case. Among the first reforms introduced after the Crown assumed the government of India were the introduction of civil, penal, and criminal codes, 1859-1861, which were explicit and tailored to Indian circumstances. The principal additions thereafter included more than a dozen acts introduced between 1908 and the 1930s, which provided the formal basis for combating nationalist activity. The 1950 constitution of independent India stipulated that previous laws, including colonial ones, would remain in effect until modified. The 1948 West Bengal Criminal Code was mainly a rewriting of colonial law, and in the same year the West Bengal Security Act reestablished legal tools, including preventive detention, which the British had used to combat nationalism. Fragmentary evidence suggests that severe penalties were prescribed in the law administered by the East India Company, whereas the 1859-1861 codes reflected the somewhat less punitive orientation of prevailing English criminal law. There has been no subsequent easing of sanctions, however: Both capital and corporal punishment continue to be administered in independent India.

The evolution of Swedish criminal law appears to have been a more orderly process than was found in the English tradition, if only because it was punctuated by three comprehensive recodifications, the first in 1734. But the difference is more apparent than real because most of the substantive and procedural changes in Swedish law have been introduced piecemeal; the recodifications of 1865 and 1965 were consolidations rather than fundamental innovations. The eighteenth century code resembled English law in its reliance on the threat of death to restrain offenders—there were 68 capital offenses, including many kinds of theft. Torture and other forms of corporal punishment also were prescribed. Liberalization of punishment began earlier than in England; the use of the death penalty was significantly limited in 1779 and abolished for most other offenses in the 1850s. Only fifteen executions took place after 1865, and the penalty was taken off the books in 1921. The comparatively early decline in reliance on capital and corporal punishment in Sweden was paralleled by the expansion of legally prescribed options for treatment, as reviewed in a subsequent chapter.

DEFINING DISORDER: ELITE INTERESTS AND SOCIAL ISSUES

The foregoing chronicle of changes may obscure recognition that the nineteenth century was the principal era of rationalization and consolidation in criminal law in all four societies. The basic definitions of individual criminal behavior that apply today were largely established in the years between 1825 and 1885. But the generalization does not extend to the regulation of collective behavior, and it masks considerable variation in the definition of particular kinds of offenses. We focus more closely now on historical changes in the nature and especially the scope of formal definitions of "criminal" behavior. Such changes reflect evolving social interests in public order, as we have observed. They also potentially influence the volume of reported crime, the number of persons prosecuted, and the burden on penal and rehabilitative institutions: As the boundaries of criminal behavior expand, more people and activities are subject to arrest and sanction, and vice versa. The comparisons to follow deal with the nature and social origins of definitional change; institutional embodiments and consequences are examined subsequently.

"Common Crime"

The legal definitions of murder, assault, rape, malicious destruction of property, and similar crimes of aggression have changed little during the last two centuries in the societies investigated. But there has been some expansion in the social groups and circumstances to which the definitions apply: Attacks on and physical abuse of "natives," servants, employees, wives, children, and inmates are more likely to be specified in law as criminal offenses now than in 1800. Special status for superordinates in criminal matters was long a feature of law in medieval and renaissance Europe. Even in the sixteenth century the upper classes of some European societies continued to enjoy the privilege of carrying on feuds, and under cover of these legal hostilities they used to hire people to commit acts of assault and robbery that were capital offenses when indulged in by members of subordinate classes. The reduction of such privileges for powerful groups was part of a broader movement to reduce the imprecision of criminal law and the arbitrariness of its application. The movement arose in the eighteenth century, stimulated by the intellectual thought of the Enlightenment and by the interests of the rising middle classes in securing their rights vis à vis their rulers.[4] The "rationalization" of criminal law was one manifestation of this movement; there were many others as well and in fact the desire for fairness and exactitude underlies many of the reforms in policing and judicial and penal policies to be cited presently.

While old immunities have been dissolved by the principle of equality before the law, new forms of aggressive and acquisitive behavior have inspired legal modernization. Some additions have been devised in response to the evolving technology of mayhem, giving police and courts the authority to sanction the carrying and use of razors, firearms, bombs, and so forth. But these are essentially new means of regulating behaviors whose general character has been long proscribed; they are responses to the changing "opportunity structure" for physical attack. More substantial modifications in the criminal law governing theft have the same kind of origin. Because of economic and technological change, there are new things to be stolen; hence criminal codes have been elaborated to prohibit, for example, the theft of bicycles, autos, aircraft, bank notes, securities, and credit cards. In addition, new and more devious ways of stealing things have inspired a great expansion of criminal laws bearing on fraud, embezzlement, and other white-collar crimes. But these changes signify no alteration of the basic principle that personal, commercial, and public property is supposed to be secure from seizure by force, stealth, or subterfuge. This principle is the basis of the contemporary criminal codes of all Western societies and most others.

We note one small step that may portend the decriminalization of some kinds of theft, however. In Sweden in 1971 an official commission coupled a recommendation that penalties for petty shoplifting be reduced with the proposal that merchants warn first offenders rather than report them to the police. In 1974 the police were instructed not to record thefts from stores with a value of less than 20 kronor (about $5 U.S.) nor to arrest their perpetrators. Many different strands of social change come together in this small innovation. One is the long-standing trend toward "liberalization" in Swedish criminal law and treatment, another is the general prosperity of Swedish society (i.e., commercial victims of $5 thefts are not seriously discommoded). The effect of the Swedish policy is to give the sanction of law to a prevalent commercial practice in other Western societies—to accept the costs of pilferage and pass them on as a kind of generalized tax to consumers. A third feature of the Swedish policy is that it relieves the bureaucracy of the burden of dealing with a host of petty matters at a time when more serious offenses also have increased substantially. The Swedish policy may have some appeal to hard-pressed officials and intellectual reformers. If applied in less egalitarian and prosperous societies, however, its effect would be a regressive "tax" on those least able to afford it. In the United States it is the urban poor who are most victimized by theft and high prices.

Social Conduct

The legal regulation of social conduct has varied more in the last two centuries than has the regulation of assault and theft, especially in the three Western societies. Control of employment and unemployment was of serious concern to the propertied classes of European societies during the eighteenth and nineteenth centuries, and class economic interests are clearly evident in much of the applicable criminal legislation. In England the Masters and Servants Acts, of medieval origin but much revised, prescribed criminal penalties for workers who broke contracts or left work unfinished; they were widely used in the early nineteenth century, notably against workers who resisted the reductions in their wages that were a consequence of the labor surplus of the period. These acts remained on the books in vestigial form even after a reforming act in 1875. Of the same genre was the Masters and Servants Act of 1828 in New South Wales, which was enacted during a severe labor shortage and created the offenses of neglect of work, absence from work, and the destruction or loss of an employer's property. Another body of relevant legislation having an equally ancient pedigree was aimed at vagrancy, that is, lack of regular employment. The first English legislation on the subject dates from 1349, with numerous subsequent modifications. In 1743 legislation broadened the definition of people who could be treated as vagrants, the Vagrancy Act of 1824 added new penalties, the Vagrancy Act of 1935 modified them. Initially such laws were used in combination with workhouses to provide relief for the poor;

later, especially in the eighteenth and nineteenth centuries, they were relied on for social control of the classes thought to be dangerous. Generally the vagrancy laws of the nineteenth century had the effect of obliging the lower classes to accept private employment on any terms or be forced into public employment. An example from New South Wales is an act of 1835 that created a whole range of "idle and disorderly" offenses, for which the penalties were terms at hard labor—the penal practice being to hire out such individuals to private employers. In Sweden during the same period the authorities were especially concerned about the costs, and the strife potential, of rampant unemployment in Stockholm. A half dozen ordinances requiring military service, and later forced labor, for those without other means of support were passed between 1802 and 1846. In the latter part of the nineteenth century vagrancy was made a civil rather than a criminal matter, but this meant in practice that administrative bodies could—and regularly did—intern vagrants in agricultural colonies. Laws against vagrancy were still being applied in Sweden in the 1920s, though apprehensions by then were but a tenth of what they had been 50 years earlier.

Another facet of social conduct much subject to regulation in these societies is the use of alcohol and drugs. It is possible to impute economic motives to these efforts on the argument that intoxicated people make poor workers, but there are more potent and direct explanations. From the official point of view drunkenness has been a nuisance, to say the least. It was and is a chronic source of private brawls and attacks on police, and during the periods for which arrests data are available, it usually has been the single most common offense in all three Western cities. From a social welfare perspective alcoholism was devastating to the family life of its victims, and members of large and broadly based prohibition movements in the three Western societies in the nineteenth and early twentieth centuries sought to reduce these costs.

Efforts at the control of alcohol abuse in this period did not elicit major changes in the scope of the criminal law, however, because being drunk and disorderly was a criminal offense virtually throughout the period and new legislation affected mainly private distilling, bootlegging, and the retail trade. In New South Wales controls on the liquor trade were established in the earliest days of the colony. The heyday of the prohibition movement in the 1880s saw some expansion of administrative restraints (fewer licensed public bars, Sunday closing laws), but neither then nor later has the relevant law been substantially modified. The Swedish emphasis also has been on drying up the source of the problem, beginning with prohibition of household distilling early in the last century, restrictions on numbers of taverns, the establishment of a state monopoly on retail sale of liquor, and rationing from the 1920s to 1955. The temperance movement, begun in the 1830s, actively promoted its policies for a century but failed to secure complete prohibition in a national referendum in 1922.

The Swedish approach to drunkenness differs in emphasis from the prevailing official view in England and the antipodes, where public drunkenness is treated first and last as a criminal offense. In Sweden, though a major emphasis of law and policy since the 1920s has been to treat and rehabilitate alcoholics, arrest rates continue at a very high level in Stockholm because not all drunks are alcoholics. The Swedish preference for decriminalization was evident in the end of rationing in 1955, which was expected to end widespread but small-scale bootlegging. Judging from arrest data it seems to have stimulated bootlegging instead, and it certainly contributed to a marked increase in arrests for drunkenness thereafter. Drunken driving, however, has been a criminal offense since 1934. Moreover the scope of the relevant law has been increased by extending it to moped drivers (1952) and by reducing the threshold of blood alcohol concentration required for criminal sanctions (1941, 1957). Imprisonment is mandatory for most drunken driving offenses, and ten percent of those in prison on any given day in contemporary Sweden are there for that reason.

Regulation of the use of drugs other than alcohol has been a more recent development. The first major English legislation dates from 1920. In Sweden, incremental controls on prescriptions and on other facets of drug use began in the late 1930s and were extended in the next two decades. The growth of drug use in the late 1960s stimulated new narcotics legislation in 1968 and 1969, significantly broadening the scope of related offenses and prescribing penalties that are quite severe by contemporary Swedish standards. It is evident from this example, and also from the Swedish policy of mandatory jail sentences for drunken driving, that whereas Swedish law and society may be "tolerant" about sex and theft, other kinds of deviance meet a firm legal and penal response.

Sexual behavior is the last area of social conduct to be considered here. The legal description of "sex crimes" has changed unmistakably over time in the Western societies. Male homosexuality, a criminal offense of long standing in all three was decriminalized in Sweden in 1944 and in England in 1967; but this move has not been made in New South Wales. Prostitution per se has never been an offense in England and Sweden, but it has been the object of a great deal of law-making and regulatory activity. The English approach was to restrict prostitution by imposing criminal penalties on soliciting, procuring, brothel keeping, and other ancillary activities. A high pitch of public morality was reached in 1885 when a consolidating act was passed by Parliament to close loopholes in earlier statutes; further restrictions were imposed by acts of 1912, 1922, and 1959. The Swedish approach emphasized regulation rather than criminalization, though in Stockholm as in London procuring and brothel keeping were criminal offenses. Regulation in Stockholm took the form of obligatory registration and medical checkups, practices in force for most of the nineteenth century. Prostitutes who failed to register or violated regulations (e.g., by wearing sensational clothing) were subject to criminal penalties. In this century the trend in Stockholm has been toward deregulation and decriminalization. Police registration of prostitutes ended in 1918, and a program to control venereal disease was established. The Vagrancy Act was applied to prostitutes during the next decade, but since 1930 the official policy has been one of toleration. During the same era, from the second to fourth decades of the century, adultery and other kinds of consensual sexual activities were also decriminalized.

The New South Wales experience again offers a sharp contrast. The nineteenth-century legal strictures on sexual behavior were substantial and emphasized criminal sanctions rather than regulation. In this century new sex-related offenses have been added, and there has been no legal decriminalization. A 1967 act, for example, establishes criminal penalties for those frequenting premises used by prostitutes, as well as for prostitution in massage parlors. Most laws related to sexual conduct seem to be enforced more selectively now than they were in the past, but there is persisting political and official resistance to formal decriminalization.

Abortion is another aspect of sex-related behavior that has generated considerable social debate, criminal legislation, and official action in all the Western societies. In England the termination of pregnancy was made an offense punishable by life imprisonment in 1861. In the 1920s abortion was sanctioned in cases where the mother's life was endangered. Proabortion groups secured the liberalization of the law in practice in the late 1930s, but not until 1967 were the legal grounds expanded significantly. In Sweden abortion was regarded as a very serious offense during the nineteenth and early twentieth centuries, and the first step toward decriminalization was not made until 1939. Since then the trend has been to increase the circumstances under which legal abortions can be obtained. One important expansion occurred in 1968; seven years later abortion by a licensed practitioner during the first trimester was entirely decriminalized. In New South Wales, interestingly, there was little public or official concern with abortion until the turn of the century, when a number of "abortion scandals" were denounced by press and from pulpit, and an official commission blamed the state's decline in birthrate on contraception and abortion. A spate of legislation accompanied this public furor, in which abortion and related activities (advertising abortion services, selling abortion-inducing drugs, etc.) were criminalized. These activities, like most other crimes of social conduct in New South Wales, have not come to the point of formal decriminalization.

Other significant areas of social conduct that are sometimes subject to criminal law have not been discussed here. One is public behavior: Numerous statutes in the Western cities prohibit a variety of raucous, insulting, and indecent actions. Anxiety over such conduct increased markedly during the nineteenth century, mainly as a reflection of evolving middle-class concern about decorous behavior, and the prohibiting laws generally remain in force. Two areas that merit more serious attention are traffic and commerce. The first is the object of familiar regulations about who can drive what, where, and how; trade and banking activities come under a host of mainly administrative regulations about who can sell what to whom, from what premises under what terms and circumstances. We have not separately analyzed these spheres of official action, or similar ones, because they have rarely posed critical issues for the public or officials in the societies we studied. They are part of the more or less routine control that has become essential to the functioning of complex societies. From a general perspective on public order, though, they may deserve more attention than we have given them. The number and scope of traffic and commerce regulations has expanded exponentially over time, and their net effect in restraining human behavior and interaction is no doubt much greater—because they affect more people more of the time—than all the body of law relating to common crime and social deviance. Moreover if such regulatory activities were curtailed or suspended, the unbridled interests of drivers and businessmen, among others, would very likely give rise to nasty and pervasive social problems that in turn would generate substantial pressures for the restoration of "public order."

Nothing has been said here about the regulation of social conduct in Calcutta. Although our sources make frequent references to attempts to regulate public behavior and commercial activity of the types just mentioned, there is little evidence that questions of sexual morality ever occasioned a great deal of legislative or official concern.

Collective Behavior

The legal definitions of assault, theft, and similar crimes have been modernized and rationalized during the past 150 years, but the underlying legal conception of violations of person and property is little changed. "Criminal" social conduct has varied more widely in definition, among and within societies, mainly in response to changing middle-class and official perceptions of vital social and moral issues. The most distinctive indications of changing class interest in public order, though, are apparent in the shifting legal ground rules of permissible collective behavior. There is a pattern of spasmodic legal response by dominant social groups to threatening collective behavior from others, followed in the Western societies by political accommodation that is reflected in legal reform.

An enduring feature of the legal codes of virtually all Western societies is a set of statutes authorizing officials to control such collective actions as riotous behavior, unlawful assembly, and acts of mutiny, rebellion, and sedition. Some of the variation in these legal controls is a function of the development of new repressive means. Yet most changes sharpen and expand, or contract, the definitions of criminal collective behavior, in response to the emergence of new forms and methods of dissent and opposition. Growing use of sabotage by English workers and Irish nationalists, for example, promoted the passage of the Malicious Damage Act of 1861. This law imposed severe penalties for causing damage with explosives, and for a wide range of other actions that previously had not required itemization: setting fire to churches, flooding mines, damaging quays and locks, and destroying bridges. Instead of reviewing all instances of legal response to collective behavior in the four societies, we present sketches of the legal efforts to control the activities of organized labor in England, mainly in the nineteenth century, and the legal manifestations of the colonial authorities' response to nationalism in Bengal in the twentieth century.

The emergent trade unions of eighteenth century England began as local "clubs" or "societies" and were tolerated as long as they remained parochial in scope, making no demands of employers. If they united over larger areas (hence the word "union"), they were very likely to encounter legal and judicial repression. The same kinds of response usually met protests over wage rates, which by custom were sometimes directed at magistrates (who traditionally regulated wages) and the House of Commons, as well as at employers. By the end of the century some forty acts prohibited workers' organizations in particular trades. Concerted legislative action was first taken in the Combination Acts of 1799 and 1800, which prescribed a general "remedy." The penalty for a first offense was "three months in gaol, or two months' hard labour [for] any working man who combined with another to gain an increase in wages or a decrease in hours, or solicited anyone else to leave work, or objected to working with any other workmen."[5] It is worth pointing out that the immediate occasion for the 1799 act was a petition by master millwrights to the House of Commons seeking the suppression of a combination of millwrights in the London area; though no more threatening than many past instances, the circumstances coincided with a "reformist" interest in Parliament to deal in a general and systematic way with a problem previously treated piecemeal. Whereas the Combination Acts were indicative of a rationalizing spirit rather than a change in social or political interest, their repeal 24 years later was the result of the actions of a group of radical members of Parliament. The repeal, which spurred an almost instant explosion of trade unionism, and also strikes, was promptly amended (in 1825) to restrict the activities of the unions, but not to outlaw them again. The trend from then to the present century was one of gradual expansion of the rights of organized workers, punctuated by episodes of increased restraint. Picketing, decriminalized by an act of 1859, was effectively criminalized again—along with other strike actions—in the early 1870s. Later acts resumed the liberalizing trend; one in 1875 made an employee's breach of contract a civil rather than criminal matter. The right to strike was significantly expanded in 1906 by the new Liberal Government, and in 1913 the Liberals also legalized political action by trades unions.

It is important to note that the gradual decriminalization of labor activism in England was not the work of working-class representatives in Parliament; the Labour Party elected its first MPs in 1906 and formed its first government in 1924. Reform was mainly the work of middle-class politicians who were sympathetic to workers' interests and demands and also concerned with general issues of social and economic progress. Their objectives were not to pave the way for working-class political control or state socialism—outcomes most of them would have abhorred—but rather to improve the operation of the capitalist system. Moreover there were limits to the kind of collective action that the elite was prepared to tolerate from workers. The London police went on strike in August 1918, and the next year Parliament passed an act prohibiting trade unionism among the police. A protest strike by the London police was crushed, as was their union. In 1927, the year after the Great Strike virtually paralyzed British industry, a Conservative Government passed a Trade Disputes and Trade Unions Act specifying heavy penalties for general and sympathy strikes and restricting picketing. In contemporary Britain it is a matter of paramount importance to restrain wage demands and limit local, unsanctioned ("wildcat") strikes. The necessity of limiting the scope of collective action by workers is accepted even by Labour Governments, but the use of criminal law and penalties to attain that end has fallen into disrepute.

In Bengal the demands of Indian nationalists in the twentieth century were intrinsically more extreme than the demands of English labor, and the British legal responses to them were comparably harsher and less compromising. Table II.3.1 shows more clearly than a narrative account the timing of major episodes of nationalist activity in Bengal and additions to Bengal and Indian law between 1906 and 1946. Three general observations may be made about the information summarized there. First, the correlation in timing between peaks of strife and legal response is approximate rather than precise partly because some of the legal response was aimed at all-India problems rather than those of Bengal specifically.

Second, there are several dimensions to the legal response: (1) control of the propagation of nationalist sentiments, (2) expansion of police powers, (3) expansion of judicial and penal procedures, especially the use of special tribunals and preventive detention, and (4) limits on certain kinds of collective behavior, public meetings in particular. Only the first and last dimensions formally expanded the scope of criminal behavior; the others gave officials the means to implement repressive policies within the boundaries of old and new definitions.

The third observation is that although the policies carried out within this expanding legal framework produced some periods of respite from strife, they only postponed the nationalist victory. In the short run they sometimes seemed to work; in the long run they did not. One can only speculate whether more compromising and less repressive responses would have made any difference. Given the gulf between Indian and British values and interests, it is unlikely that accommodation would have affected the final outcome, but it would have made the struggle less costly for all concerned.

Some briefer observations about the Swedish and New South Wales experience of legal control of collective behavior conclude this section. Both governments experimented with censorship laws in the early nineteenth century to muzzle liberal criticism (Sweden 1812, New South Wales 1827). But the attempts were soon abandoned in the face of middle-class opposition. Laws aimed at suppressing labor activity in Sweden appeared mainly between 1887 and 1900 and included fresh resort to censorship. Little used after universal franchise was granted in 1921, the controls were repealed in the late 1930s. The rise of the labor movement in New South Wales generated less intense conflict than parallel developments in the other societies. Masters and servants laws against "conspiracy" to raise wages were on the books but were not updated after 1840. More to the point, there is no evidence that they were widely used to control the new labor movement. The first legislation specifically aimed at modern labor conflict, passed in 1901, required compulsory arbitration of disputes. Accommodation to early labor demands in New South Wales may be attributed to two reinforcing factors: The colony had no entrenched upper class, and labor was a scarce and

Table II.3.1 Nationalism and British Legal Response in Bengal, 1906-1946

Manifestations of nationalism	Years	Years	Additions to criminal and civil law
Agitation against partition of Bengal	1906-1908	1908	Criminal law amendment: various political organizations banned
		1910	Press Act: security deposit required for distribution of printed matter
		1910	Bengal Code Act III: public meetings limited
		1911	Prevention of Seditious Meetings Act
Intensified nationalist agitation, large-scale terrorism	1912-1915	1915	Defence of India Act: preventive detention, suspension of due process, ban on public meetings
		1919	Rowlatt Act: wide powers to control terrorism
Noncooperation movement, political strikes	1920-1924	1921	Criminal law amendment: preventive detention, control of public meetings
		1924	Criminal law amendment: greater police powers
		1924	Sea Customs Act: controls on import of seditious material
		1924	Goonda Act: deportation of known goondas [professional thugs] from Calcutta
		1926	Penal law amendment: special courts for political crimes
Large-scale political strikes	1928	1929	Press Act: security deposit required for publication
Civil disobedience movement, political strikes	1930-1934	1930	Bengal law amendment: suspension of civil rights, preventive detention
Quit India movement	1942-1943	1942	Emergency Powers Act: banning of political organization, detention of leaders
Worst communal rioting in Calcutta's history	1946	1946	Defence of India Act: expanded detention, control of subversive organizations

precious commodity. Legislation passed during World War I outlawed the International Workers of the World, not for economic reasons but because of the labor organization's outspoken pacifism. Class tensions and labor surplus increased during the Depression, and in 1929 a predominantly conservative state assembly passed punitive antistrike legislation. The immediate internal stimulus was a timber workers' strike, the external model was the repressive labor legislation passed in England 1927. Like much other criminal legislation in New South Wales, the 1929 act remained formally in force long after it ceased to be applied.

All the foregoing examples of legal response to collective behavior predate the upsurge of protest and terrorism in the past decade. The Swedish legal response is instructive, though not typical. The widespread toleration of peaceful protest in Swedish society is reflected in two recent legislative actions. Strikes by public servants were legalized in 1965. After 1970 it was no longer a criminal offense to insult Swedish or national foreign symbols nor to advocate rebellion. The net effect of the 1970 changes was to legalize political demonstrations, notably those directed at United States foreign policy since 1965. Swedish toleration of dissent stops well short of violence, however. Strict measures enacted in 1973 gave the police broad powers to deal with the terrorists, mainly Croatians and Palestinians, who had become active in Stockholm. On both these issues, innovation in Swedish law reflects not narrow class or elite interests but a broad spectrum of public opinion.

On the basis of the evidence reviewed here, criminal law represents very different sets of interests, depending on the "criminal" behavior in question. The class-interest explanation of the criminal law fits best the legislation aimed at controlling collective behavior. The changing fears and sympathies of the political elite and the rising political influence of new classes are traced in legislation governing collective behavior, as surely as a seismograph records earthquakes and tremors. The laws governing social and sexual conduct are more ambiguous cases. Most of the relevant law in Western societies is an outgrowth of historical efforts to codify the standards of middle-class morality and to apply them to all social groups. Such laws are, or were, manifestations of class social interests rather than narrowly political or economic ones. The standards applied now are not only or mainly those of the middle classes, however. Some are almost universally accepted, and one probably would find less tolerance for drug and alcohol abuse, and sexual deviance, in the working-class neighborhoods of the three Western cities than among the politicians, officials, and intellectuals of the new ruling class. Consensus was and continues to be greatest about common crimes against persons and property. No vocal group seems ever to have argued that such acts should be tolerated. The class issue with respect to these offenses has been how theft and violence should be dealt with.

NOTES TO PART II, CHAPTER 3

1. William L. Langer, "Europe's Initial Population Explosion," in Carl E. Schorske and Elizabeth Schorske, eds., *Explorations in Crisis: Papers on International History* (Cambridge: Harvard University Press, 1969), p. 439. For a comparative analysis of the consequences of this immiseration for criminal law and penal practice see Georg Rusche and Otto Kirchheimer, *Punishment and Social Structure* (New York: Columbia University Press, 1939), ch. 6.

2. The reference is to Asa Briggs, *The Age of Improvement* (London: Longmans, Green, 1959), which deals with the period 1784-1867.

3. Other common penal practices in eighteenth and early nineteenth century England were sentences to workhouses and corporal punishments such as whipping. The evolution of penal practices is examined in a subsequent chapter.

4. On these points see Rusche and Kirchheimer, op. cit., esp. pp. 15-16, 72-83. For a detailed study of English law on theft which emphasizes the social and economic circumstances of its evolution, see Jerome Hall, *Theft, Law and Society*, 2nd ed. (Indianapolis: Bobbs-Merrill, 1952).

5. A paraphrase, not a quotation from the act, from G. D. H. Cole and Raymond Postgate, *The Common People 1746-1946*, 4th ed. (London: Methuen, 1949), p. 173.

Chapter 4

THE POLICE AND POLICING

Criminal laws cannot be systematically enforced without specialized policing agencies. Such bodies can be identified in many European cities as early as medieval times, but the history of police and policing in Europe up to the nineteenth century, insofar as it is known, shows more diversity than similarity. Policing was sometimes a local sometimes a national function; usually it was carried out by organizations whose roles differed widely. Some bodies were concerned with patrolling, others with apprehending known criminals, still others (or sometimes the same ones) with controlling political dissidence and riotous crowds. Contemporary European police systems have some organizational and operational features in common, but these are more readily explained by convergence through imitative response to similar problems, especially in the last century, than by common dynamics of development. Diversity among contemporary European police systems, Bayley suggests, is due partly to the different patterns of national political conflict and development, partly to a kind of organizational inertia that permits the culturally distinctive traits of police organizations to persist over time.[1]

The institutional development of the police is important to our analysis because the quality and extent of public order, and the official indicators of disorder, depend very directly on what the police do and how they do it. At the same time we are concerned with the social and political forces that have shaped police organization and activities. Institutional changes in the police, like changes in the criminal law, are influenced by larger political and social circumstances and particularly by the shifting interests and concerns of dominant social groups. The sections that follow trace the development of police forces in the four cities with special attention to external influences on their growth and operations. Many of the characteristics of police organizations are also subject to the internal, system-maintaining dynamics of bureaucratic organizations, but they are not analyzed here; the main concern is the external sources of constraint and change.

PREMODERN URBAN POLICING

Some form of policing was carried out in all four cities from early times, but the activities were fragmented, limited in scope and function, and mostly nonprofessional. Official and public dissatisfaction culminated in major police reforms in the middle decades of the nineteenth century: in London in 1829, Stockholm in 1850, New South Wales in 1862, and Calcutta in 1864. In all four societies there were substantial changes in policing before and after the dates given, but during these years public police organizations began to acquire their contemporary forms, ethos, and methods of operation. Their prior development had been diverse and discontinuous; it became more similar and evolutionary. We begin by sketching the character of policing in the four cities before these transitions.

London, which was already a large city in the early eighteenth century, made do with uncoordinated policing arrangements at the parish level. Householders typically served as constables, and watchmen were employed and supervised by notoriously venal local justices of the peace and officers of the watch. It was regarded as a signal improvement when magistrates Henry and John Fielding, in the 1750s, established a small cadre of professional "thief-takers" who operated throughout the metropolis. Another advance occurred with the introduction of annual stipends for some justices, who had previously been subsisting on what they could extract in fees and fines from their clientele. The first professional force in London was the Marine Police Establishment, founded in 1798 by private merchants but soon taken over by the Home Office. As of 1800, when London had about 900,000 inhabitants, there were roughly 500 professional police, including the river police, the Bow Street Runners established by the Fieldings, and constables attached to district magistrates' offices, plus perhaps 4,500 watchmen at the neighborhood level. Watchmen aside, the primary task of the police was to capture known offenders. Reformers in and out of the House of Commons advanced proposals for a centralized, professional police force from the 1750s through the 1820s, on grounds that existing bodies were often corrupt and generally were ineffective in preventing crime. The proposals came to nothing, however. Two recurring themes of political opposition were the fear that the police would become an instrument of repression, and resistance to spending public funds on policing. In addition London's aldermen and magistrates were concerned about the possible loss of control of a function that traditionally had been theirs. It should be pointed out that Londoners lacked neither models nor precedent: A centralized and increasingly professional police force had functioned in Paris since the late seventeenth century, and the British government had seen to the establishment of a salaried, centralized police force in Ireland in 1786. It was the activities of these forces, especially in Paris, that inspired influential members of the urban middle classes to fear a centralized London police as a threat to their liberties.

In Stockholm, with less than a tenth of London's population, policing in 1800 was divided among a city guard of sixteenth century origin, a fire guard, and a military garrison, each having some law enforcement functions (mainly patrolling), and a newly reformed (1797) police force of about 90 men whose principal task was to arrest offenders. In 1812 the total strength of these bodies, excluding the garrison, was about 400 for a city of some 75,000. This works out to a ratio of about 50 men per 10,000 population compared with a ratio of about 55 per 10,000 in London at the same period. The major changes in policing in the first half of the century were consolidation of the fire guard and garrison into the Military Corps and increases in police patrolling. Merchants' concern about rising theft in the early 1830s inspired some of these changes; riots in 1838 were followed by the inauguration of intensive patrols by the Military Corps and, later, the opening of the first three neighborhood police stations. ·Criticism of police services was particularly pronounced in the 1830s and 1840s, partly because of high levels of public disorder, partly because the police and the Military Corps were a rough lot who used harsh methods. The reports of the governor of Stockholm in the 1840s expressed strong dissatisfaction with the Military Corps, and the liberal press was also critical; otherwise voiceless ordinary citizens expressed their antagonisms in individual and collective assaults on police and patrols.

In Sydney a night watch was established a year after the colony was founded, and in 1810 a permanent force of 35 constables was created to police a settlement of about 7,000 inhabitants. Separate forces were later set up to patrol the native population, rural and border areas, and the Sydney waterfront, and by 1850 the colony had six separate and uncoordinated forces. The City Police were very badly paid by standards of the time; many were ex-convicts, and most were untrained men who left the force after brief service. Colonial and municipal authorities contributed to these problems by curtailing police expenditures as public order improved in the 1830s; thus by 1844 the force numbered only 95 men for a booming town of some 40,000—a ratio of less than 25 per 10,000 compared with a ratio nearly double that just five years earlier. There were many demands for police reform from the 1830s on, including the recommendations of a succession of official committees. Some were inspired by relevations of corruption and incompetence on the force (three successive chiefs of police were dismissed for malfeasance), others by urban riots.

In Calcutta the first public watch force of 68 Indians was established in 1704 and was supplemented by a tiny military contingent the next year. By the beginning of the nineteenth century responsibilities for public order were divided among the river police, the boundary police, and the town guard, each with specialized duties, and the primarily Indian *thandari* force, which provided general police services. Europeans on the latter force served mainly in the city's European neighborhoods. By 1842 the Calcutta police numbered 1,838 men, sixteen of them Europeans, for a city of about a quarter million—a ratio of about 75 per 10,000. Though relatively numerous by comparison with the other cities, the Calcutta police were similarly untrained, underpaid, and unloved. Little skill could be expected of police whose wages throughout the nineteenth century were below those paid to manual laborers and whose turnover rates were 50 percent a year or more. They were known to be corrupt and brutal; police officials acknowledged widespread use of torture to secure confessions. The governor of Bengal bluntly reported in 1834 that "The whole of the police is abhorred and detested by the people. . . ." However his judgment and the criticisms and pleas of several police commissioners failed to move the East India Company to reduce its profits by increasing the funds devoted to civil administration.

These sketches illustrate a number of points about premodern police services. Their "fragmented" character, for example, reflects a contemporary value judgment. By the standards of the societies in which they evolved, they were typical of public response to social problems: Specific problems were met with specific responses; thus policing services, like criminal laws, were numerous and narrow in scope. This may throw some light on one aspect of the "modernization" process, which prevailing academic opinion holds to involve a shift from functionally diffuse to functionally specific organization. In fact eighteenth and early nineteenth century European police organizations (and many others) were a good deal more specialized in function than are modern forces. Modernization has been more a matter of coordination, integration, and professionalization than specialization.

Another distinctive characteristic of premodern police is that in most respects they were indistinguishable from those whom they policed. Police organizations were staffed by men drawn from the lowest ranks of societies, the same groups whose criminality was of greatest official concern. They were frequently corrupt, brutal, and as fond of alcohol as those whose drunkenness warranted police attention. They rarely had uniforms or special equipment, nor did they receive special training except for those enlisted in paramilitary units. The men most likely to remain on police and watch forces for any length of time were those whose personal limitations—infirmity, age, lack of skills—prevented them from taking more attractive employment. Norms of professional conduct were highly unlikely to develop and be maintained in such circumstances. It is little wonder that the police were detested and scorned by ordinary citizens.

These characteristics of premodern police cannot be explained by attributing to elites a clever scheme of setting thieves to catch thieves. Their motives, insofar as we can judge by what they said and did, were simpler: Maintaining public order was a dirty job that was to be done as cheaply as possible. Economic motives were repeatedly evident in elite decisions about policing. Where possible, the costs of policing were put off onto private citizens, merchants, and local communities, or met by paying fees to "thief-takers" (with funds derived from the confiscation of criminals' property). The police reforms of Stockholm in 1850 were financed by new taxes on the liquor trade—poetic justice, since drunks were the policeman's principal clients. When public funds had to be expended, they were grudgingly allocated and subject to pressures to cut them back.

THE TRANSITION TO MODERN POLICING

Criticisms of police services and demands for reform were common in all four societies for decades before the moves toward centralization in the 35 years between 1829 and 1864. Thus it is worth asking what kinds of circumstances contributed to reform. In three of the four societies the new forces were established in and for the capital city (the exception is New South Wales, where policing was colonywide). Only later were the new police systems extended to other cities, towns, and rural areas. Therefore it is reasonable to assume that the distinctive problems of metropolitan public order provided one incentive to reform. Which problems were most important remains to be shown, however. One possibility that can be dismissed at the outset is pressure arising from the scale and anonymity of urban life. The cities' approximate populations at the dates of transition were as follows:

Greater London, 1829:   1,800,000
Stockholm, 1850:   92,000
Sydney, 1862:   100,000 (New South Wales 370,000)
Calcutta, 1864:   365,000

There is no basis here for an argument that there exists a threshold of urban size beyond which centralized policing becomes essential. The distinctive urban problems of public order have more to do with the ideas, interests, and circumstances of urban social groups.

One source of demands for police reform was intellectual and social. The same spirit of rationalization and reform that led to legal recodification in European societies was applied to policing: The search for order and security by the urban middle classes and the political elite could not be satisfied by legal reform alone but required new and more efficient institutions capable of enforcing the new laws. The idea of professional police forces was widely advocated on the Continent, especially by those impressed with the efficacy of the French and Prussian police in maintaining political and social order. Continental visitors often expressed surprise at the toleration of the English for high levels of urban crime and vice that could easily be lowered, they thought, by police methods already in use abroad. The relative success of the English system, once inaugurated (in London in 1829, countrywide in 1839), increased the likelihood of imitation elsewhere.[2]

The middle decades of the nineteenth century brought rapid commercial expansion to all the cities. Prosperous urban merchants and middle-class householders were more numerous and had more to lose from theft than in earlier times. In London and Stockholm the middle classes also were politically more influential than their forebears had been. But there is no precise correlation between the increasing prosperity and political influence of rising classes and the timing of police innovations. These factors, like "the police idea," provided at best a general disposition to police reform, not an explanation of when or how it occurred.[3] For that we must examine specific circumstances in the four cities.

In London the fear of disorder was particularly great in the 1820s: Acquisitive and aggressive crime were thought to have increased sharply and civil strife was much feared, though little in evidence in London itself.[4] The Home Secretary, Sir Robert Peel, who earlier had supervised the Irish police and had long advocated police reform in London, was able in these circumstances to engineer parliamentary approval of an act establishing the Metropolitan Police, soon nicknamed "bobbies" or "peelers" in derisive acknowledgement of their founder. In Stockholm the telling factor was rioting in 1848, part of the wave of revolutionary and protorevolutionary activity set in motion all across the Continent by the February revolution in France. The Stockholm riots led the royal government to heed previous criticisms of the Military Corps and city police and the governor's proposals for reform. In New South Wales the final impetus for reform was not urban at all. An outbreak of bushranging and disturbances on the goldfields in 1862 gave the colonial assembly what proved to be definitive evidence of the need for an adequately financed, colonywide force. The New South Wales Police Force was established within the year, and all the Sydney police were incorporated into its Metropolitan Division. Police reorganization in Calcutta was one of the steps taken in the period of legal and penal reform that followed the introduction of royal government, that is, after the Sepoy Mutiny of 1857 had precipitated the end of private government by the East India Company. Calcutta had no immediate crisis of public order per se in the early 1860s; the principal aspect of reforms was integration of the city and suburban police under the direct authority of the government of Bengal.

We suggest, on this evidence, that crises of public order in these four societies catalyzed the implementation of police reforms that had long been sought by forward-thinking officials and, at least in the three Western cities, by some members of the middle classes. Our hypothesis is that what the middle classes wanted, and finally got, was more certain protection of person and property; what the political elite apparently desired was increased security against collective behavior by the lower classes. In support of the second part of this explanation we note that the new police forces were removed from local or metropolitan control and were made directly responsible to national or colonial governments, except in Stockholm where they continued under the governor's aegis. This is too pat to constitute a complete explanation; all the underlying intellectual, political, and economic conditions cited previously pointed in the same direction. But the evidence just reviewed makes a prima facie case that the convergence of middle-class and elite interests in the European societies eventually overcame the middle classes' fear of police forces that might be used against them, as well as both groups' reluctance to spend more public monies on routine policing.[5]

THE GROWTH OF MODERN POLICE FORCES

The new police organizations were similar in all four cities, and they followed parallel lines of development. All were centralized from the outset and were given responsibilities for policing most if not all of their metropolitan areas. All employed a precinct or district type of organization in which police were assigned to and patrolled from local station houses. The central police organizations, immediately or within a few years, assumed virtually all functions of their more specialized predecessors. Gradually they were given new responsibilities as well. Early on, all created detective branches, now much expanded, whose activities are designated "criminal investigation." Other kinds of specialized divisions were established to deal with such matters as prostitution, drugs, political dissidence, police training, communications, and traffic control. Stockholm's experience of police specialization is probably typical: In 1850 almost all its men were assigned to district patrol stations, but by 1924 its central and specialized divisions employed nearly 40 percent of the force. The Sydney and New South Wales police, who have been proportionally the smallest of the modern forces, were given especially broad responsibilities. At various times they were required to carry out such duties as licensing public houses, dogcatching, compiling electoral lists, registering motor vehicles, and counterespionage. The London police also were assigned quite broad responsibilities in the nineteenth century but later ceded many of them, not least because police commissioners complained that such tasks as the abatement of smoke nuisances and regulation of weights and measures were not properly police matters. In the present era the functions of the Stockholm police seem to be the most narrowly defined.

The new police forces absorbed not only the functions of their predecessors but many of their personnel as well, except for London where the Metropolitan Police recruited their first 1,900 men largely from the civilian population. Gradual improvements in pay and conditions of employment in the three Western forces, plus the zealous professionalism of the new police officials, led to improvement in the character and abilities of men recruited and retained in the ranks. Internal training programs for recruits began to appear later in the nineteenth century (in Stockholm in 1876; in England not until 1907). One immediate consequence of modernization was a shrinkage in the absolute number of police, but the long-run trend has been a tremendous increase in police manpower in all the cities. The data in Table II.4.1 show that all have doubled and redoubled since their reformation, and the Sydney force is 27 times as large now as it was a century ago. The police services of all these cities are now large-scale bureaucratic organizations.

The strength of police forces is usually compared in proportion to the population they control. The ratios in Table II.4.2 show that police reform invariably had the effect of reducing the relative size of police forces. In the three Western cities the force ratios had declined by 1870 to less than half their levels at the beginning of the century. It also is evident that the Western cities have had approximately similar police-to-population ratios in different eras. As best we can tell from imprecise data, all had about 50 police per 10,000 population in the early nineteenth century, and all the twentieth century ratios given are between sixteen and 33 per 10,000. Calcutta offers a substantial contrast. In both centuries its police force has been proportionally larger than any of the others.

Table II.4.1 Police Manpower in Four Cities, 1800 to 1970[a]

Time	London	Stockholm	Sydney	Calcutta
Nineteenth century First quarter	5,000[b] (1800)	400[a] (1812)	35	No data
Second quarter	4,500[b,c] (1830)	390 (1850)	114 (1839)	1,838 (1842)
1870	9,160	314	180	3,434
Twentieth century 1920	21,546	903	1,508	5,314
1970	17,380	2,435	4,862 (1969)	18,628 (1966)

a. Solid bars signify the occurrence of comprehensive police reform.
b. Estimates.
c. Including 3,000 men of the Metropolitan Police Force, an estimated 1,000 watchmen in the City of London, and an estimated 500 constables plus Thames River Police.

Table II.4.2 Police per 10,000 Population in Four Cities, 1800-1970[a]

Time	London	Stockholm	Sydney	Calcutta[b]
Nineteenth century First quarter	55[b,c] (1800)	53[b,c] (1812)	50[b] (1810)	No data
Second quarter	24[c] (1830)	42.4 (1850)	33[b] (1839)	74[b] (1842)
1870	25.3	23.1	13.3	65[b]
Twentieth century 1920	29.7	21.6	16.7	59[b]
1970	21.4	32.9	17.9 (1969)	62[b] (1966)

a. Solid bars signify the occurrence of comprehensive police reform.
b. Population data are estimated or of questionable reliability.
c. Police data are estimated.

The easiest explanation for the decline in police size following modernization is "efficiency." Integrated and professional police forces needed less manpower to carry out their duties. But economic factors also were at work, because the modernized police imposed a greater burden on the public purse than their predecessors. Pay tended to be higher, and there was substantially greater investment in training, facilities, and equipment. There also is recurring evidence that politicians and officials tried to keep postmodernization police costs down. In the Western cities, in short, reform may have bought more professional police services, but it also bought fewer police. The Calcutta police, by contrast, continued to rely on large numbers of men employed at the lowest possible wage. A series of critical government reports in the colonial period and the fiscal data of

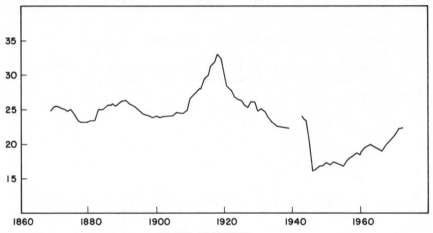

Figure II.4.1 London: Police per 10,000, 1869-1972

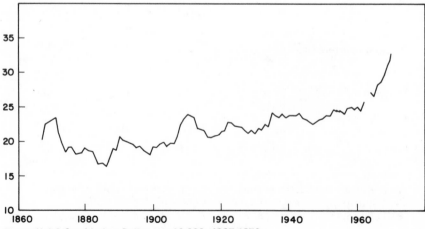

Figure II.4.2 Stockholm: Police per 10,000, 1867-1970

Calcutta police reports testify that the great bulk of the force continued to consist of untrained and underpaid Indians. In the years following independence, perhaps a third of the Calcutta police have been kept as an armed reserve to deal with civil strife. This circumstance helps account for the continued high level of police manpower, yet fragmentary data on police finances indicate that costs, hence wages and investment in training or facilities, remain low.

More precise evidence on the changing size of the urban police forces during the last century is provided in Figures II.4.1 through

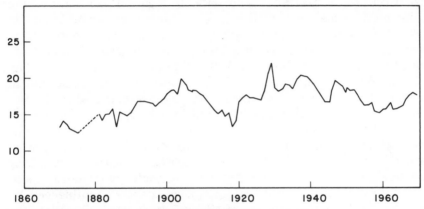

Figure II.4.3 Sydney: Police per 10,000, 1869-1969

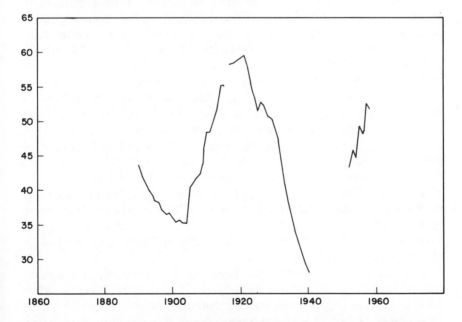

Figure II.4.4 Calcutta: Police per 10,000, 1870, 1890-1940, scattered years 1952-1966

II.4.4. There are persisting pressures, especially from the police services themselves, to increase the number of police commensurate with urban growth and police specialization. Despite these pressures for continuity, all cities record substantial and sometimes abrupt changes in ratios of police to population. Both the trends and the timing of the highs and lows differ greatly from one city to another and are suggestive about the impact of public disorder on urban policing.

In London the Metropolitan Police varied little in proportional size from 1870 to 1909. (The data in Figure II.4.1 refer to the uniformed force only.) The one notable expansion came in 1882-1884 and followed a marked increase in concern about property crime: Between 1876 and 1882, convictions for burglary and robbery and for petty theft per 100,000 population had increased by 75 and 50 percent, respectively. The most dramatic expansion in the London police in the last century, though, occurred in the five years after 1909. The absolute and proportional increases both exceeded twenty percent and coincided with the peak of the suffragette campaigns in London and the highest level of strike activity in two decades.[6] The strength of the force continued to grow during the war years, but after the Armistice it gradually declined in size (absolutely as well as proportionally), apparently uninfluenced by widespread labor turmoil in 1919-1921 and 1926. By 1946 the Metropolitan Police had fewer than 13,000 uniformed men, compared with 22,000 in 1919. Since 1946 there has been a gradual increase in the relative size of the uniformed force; the greatest absolute increases were in 1946-1948 (10 percent) and 1955-1971 (25 percent). Both were periods of rising crime rates—the first one temporary, the second coinciding with London's highest levels of civil strife in the twentieth century. Even so, the uniformed force as of 1974 was smaller, absolutely and proportionally, than it had been in the orderly days of the 1930s, and it was well below its authorized strength, as it had been for 30 years. A more telling indicator of police concern with crime was the increase of the Criminal Investigation Department (CID) from a strength of about 1,300 during the 1940s and 1950s to 3,500 in 1974. All periods of substantial increase in the size of the London police prove to have been periods of rising crime, strife, or both; and of five periods of marked increase in the two kinds of disorder in the past century, four coincided with increases in police strength.

In Stockholm the long-term trend in proportional police manpower has been upward, with a particularly sharp increase after 1961. Some of this growth was incremental; more was the result of five unmistakable short-term increases in the absolute size of the force in 1886-1890 (40 percent), 1904-1910 (32 percent), 1918-1922 (14 percent), 1928-1935 (27 percent), and 1965-1970 (16 percent). The last increase occurred while the city was losing population to suburban growth. In the late 1870s and early 1880s Stockholm experienced a substantial (40-60 percent) increase in reports of and convictions for theft, assault, and disorderly conduct, all of which declined sharply after 1886. Labor unrest also was significant in the 1880s but not a great deal more than previously. The four most conflictive periods in twentieth century Stockholm were 1904-1909 (strikes and demands for suffrage), 1916-1920 (strikes, political demonstrations, food riots), 1924-1932 (strikes, more serious elsewhere than in Stockholm), and 1965 to the present. The most substantial increases in common crime in this century occurred in 1917-1919 and from 1955 to the present. The correlation between crises of public order, especially civil strife, and enlargement of the Stockholm police is precise.

The trend in Sydney police manpower has been more variable, almost cyclical. The force increased in proportional size from the 1870s until 1904, declined until 1918, increased by more than 50 percent to 1929, then declined irregularly until about 1960, when it began to increase once again. Similar peaks and valleys are evident in the data for the entire New South Wales force (not given). The periods of greatest absolute increase in the Sydney police were 1875-1881 (73 percent), 1889-1892 (30 percent), 1918-1929 (116 percent), 1945-1947 (21 percent), and 1963-1969 (28 percent). No pronounced increase in either crime or strife preceded or coincided with the years 1875-1881. Large-scale protest by organized labor emerged between 1885 and 1890, the 1890 strike being particularly severe. The most intense periods of civil strife in twentieth century Sydney were from 1917 to 1920 and from 1926 to the early 1930s. There was no consequential increase in serious crime or strife in the mid-1940s. The rise of crime and political demonstrations in the 1960s has been documented. In Sydney the correspondence between crises of public order and expansion of the police is not as precise as in London and Stockholm, but it is substantial nonetheless.

The size of the Calcutta police force varied with remarkable regularity during the colonial period. After centralization in 1864 the police-to-population ratios declined steadily until 1904, when the force was about ten percent smaller in absolute numbers and 40 percent smaller in proportion to population than it had been in 1870. Then, in lockstep with rising Bengali nationalism, the force was swiftly and regularly increased through 1917, by 73 percent in absolute numbers. In the next two decades the city's population more than doubled, but since no increments were made to the force, by 1940 the force ratios were half what they had been in the early 1920s. The inference is that the British chose to rely on means other than police manpower to deal with endemic disorder; we have already commented on their use of emergency powers, detention camps, and troops to quell the most serious outbreaks of strife. There are two different, fragmentary series of postindependence data for Calcutta; neither is directly comparable to the earlier figures but both show a distinct proportional (and absolute) increase. The data appear to indicate attempts by government to control resurgent strife; there is no recorded evidence of a concurrent increase in crime.

Thus for the four cities in the century beginning about 1870 we have identified sixteen periods in which police manpower increased at a much greater rate than urban population: four in London, five in Stockholm, five in Sydney, and two in Calcutta. In only two cases had there been no prior or concurrent increase in civil strife or recorded crime. In three other instances police manpower was increased following an increase in crime alone, and in six cases manpower was strengthened during or immediately after a period of increased strife. In the five remaining instances the manpower increase followed or coincided with a simultaneous rise in crime and strife. It could be argued in principle that augmentations in police strength lead to increases in reported crime and stimulate popular resistance. The data are not consistent with this kind of explanation, because in virtually every instance of correlation between increased disorder and an increase in police, disorder came first. In the case of strife there is typically a year's lag between a major episode and police expansion; the indicators for crime usually register increases for five years or more before police expansion. It is not necessary to base the argument solely on temporal correlations, either. In a number of instances we have statements of contemporary officials and others that the police were expanded in response to rising disorder. The sequence is best documented for the expansion of police forces in the three Western cities in the 1960s.

There is one paradoxical aspect of this evidence. The primary rationale and duty of urban police forces is to control crime, whereas more of the police expansions have occurred in response to strife (eleven of sixteen) than to crime (eight of sixteen). To resolve the paradox, we suggest that collective disorder is more threatening to elites than is crime, and this discrepancy has been sufficient to render elites more willing to invest additional resources in standby forces that can be used for crowd control than in manpower for crime control per se.

THE EFFECTS OF POLICE REFORM
ON PUBLIC ORDER

The circumstances of police reform and expansion provide consistent and convincing evidence that these changes were intended to improve public order during years when influential social groups felt particularly threatened by rising strife and crime. But whether public order improved as a consequence is not nearly as certain. A number of factors combine to make the matter problematical.

The control of strife has been one apparent object of police expansion, but since urban strife is episodic by its nature, the passing of a particular crisis is inevitable and might be attributed to almost any prior change in circumstance or policy. In any event officials and groups who are threatened by strife are likely to regard police success in minimizing its disruptive consequences as an improvement in public order. Therefore the criteria of successful control lie in the characteristics and consequences of strife as much as in its occurrence. By this kind of standard, on the whole, the modern police in the Western cities have been quite successful. Except for incidents in Stockholm in the mid-nineteenth century, there have been virtually no instances of protracted or widespread rioting, crowds have never threatened to topple a political regime, and the police have rarely inflicted serious or fatal injuries in conflict situations. The typical police role has been to restrain crowds of demonstrators and strikers, and to disperse rioters, with a minimum of force. The success of the police in the Western cities is due partly to the circumspection of those they are attempting to control, partly to police confidence that force displayed, but used in moderation, will work in crowd-control situations. This is one of the principal consequences of police modernization and expansion for public order in these three cities; the modern police are sufficiently numerous, well-trained, and confident of their abilities to have been able to control collective protest without using force in ways that would discredit them or intensify opposition.

In contrast, we have the failure of police policies in Calcutta to control either nationalist resistance or communal rioting during the last 40 years of colonial rule. The Calcutta police, though more numerous than their European counterparts, were badly trained. The critical limitation on their performance, however, was the fact that they served illegitimate masters. The political liabilities under which they operated all but assured the failure of any meliorative influence that might have followed from police reform and expansion. If the London, Stockholm, or New South Wales police had operated in similar political circumstances, it is not likely that they would have fared better.

The problems of assessing the impact of policing on crime are still more difficult. Expansion of police manpower may lead to detection of more crime and to more arrests, thereby masking evidence of deterrent effects. Changes of crime indicators in either direction after a manpower increase may be attributable to social and economic reasons quite unrelated to increased policing. It is also possible that criminal behavior is more influenced by what police do than by their numbers or organization. Our data about changing police procedures are insufficient to permit assessment of such an explanation. Nonetheless there is enough evidence to make some limited but suggestive comparisons of the impact of police reform and expansion on crime rates.

The years of nineteenth century police reform and subsequent periods of rapid police expansion in the three Western societies provide a set of seventeen social experiments whose impact on crime rates can be compared by examining the short-term trends in summary indicators of aggressive and acquisitive crimes during and after these police changes. In the case of reforms the trend was observed during the subsequent five years. For example, the Stockholm police were reformed in 1850. Our test of the effect on crime rates is to calculate and average separately the annual rates of change in convictions per 100,000 for assaults and for thefts between 1850 and 1854. In the case of expansions we use overlapping periods, beginning with the first year of increased police strength and continuing for two years beyond. The first pronounced increase in the Stockholm force occurred in 1886-1890; our measures of effect are the average of annual rates of change in convictions per 100,000 for assaults and theft, separately, between 1887 (the first year in which any effect might be expected) and 1892 (two years after the last year of expansion). For London and New South Wales we used indicators of serious (indictable) crimes of aggression and acquisition. Because of varying availability of crime data, all pre-1940 tests use convictions per 100,000; tests after 1940 use crime known to police per 100,000. When both kinds of data were available, we made separate tests of effects (not reported here) and found them to be consistently in the same direction and of similar magnitudes.

As Table II.4.3 indicates, the principal police reforms in the nineteenth century ordinarily were followed by increased convictions. The reorganized police evidently were more zealous than their predecessors in arresting offenders. Committals to trial increased as a consequence (not shown), and so did convictions. The nine significant expansions of police strength between 1870 and 1940 had quite different kinds of results. They rarely were followed by increases in convictions; in most instances the indicators of one or both kinds of crime declined substantially thereafter.[7] One might conclude from these findings that the effect of increased policing on public order was what officials and ordinary citizens expected it to be. Since 1940, however, there has been a distinct reversal. In only two of ten comparisons was police expansion followed by a significant decline in recorded crime. In the others crime indicators continued to rise. This does not mean that increased policing is likely to have "caused" the concurrent increase, however. Most of the manpower increases in question occurred in the 1960s, and all were designed to cope with crime rates that had been rising for some years; our results for 1941-1970 simply reflect the fact that increased police manpower did not affect the rising trend.

The short-term effects of improved policing on crime (indicators of crime) differ from one time and circumstance to another. One interpretation of the findings cited is that the reformed police of the nineteenth century were in fact effective in creating public order,

Table II.4.3 The Effects of Police Reform and Expansion on Crime Indicators in London, Stockholm, and New South Wales

Average annual change in crime indicators[a]	Number of expansions		
	1829-1862[b]	1870-1940[c]	1941-1970[d]
Greater than 7% increase	3		4
4-6% increase	2	1	1
1-3% increase		2	3
No significant change		3	
1-3% decrease	1	4	
4-6% decrease		5	1
Greater than 7% decrease		3	1
Mean change[e]	+10.0%	−3.9%	−3.8%

a. Changes in indicators of aggressive and acquisitive crimes are examined and counted separately (see text).

b. Percent changes in convictions per 100,000 in the five years following police reform in London (1829), Stockholm (1850), and New South Wales (1862).

c. Percent changes in convictions per 100,000 during and immediately after years of rapid police expansion, nine instances (see text).

d. Percent changes in reported crimes per 100,000 during and immediately after years of rapid police expansion, five instances (see text).

e. Mean of averages for all recorded instances.

and the experience of the last several decades is the result of a basic change in social causality or in the institutions of public order themselves.

We earlier showed that the long-term trends in crimes of violence and theft in all three societies are remarkably similar; they declined irregularly but persistently from high levels in the second quarter of the nineteenth century to much lower levels in the 1920s and 1930s. Yet only in London did the modernization of the police in 1829 correspond approximately with the beginning of decline. Convictions for serious assaults declined by half in the two ensuing decades; indictable thefts did not taper off noticeably until after 1850. In Stockholm and New South Wales the decline came first, then police reform. Police reform in Stockholm was in fact followed by a temporary abatement of decline. In New South Wales convictions per 100,000 declined at a rate ten times as great in the two decades before police reform in 1862 as they did in the two decades after.

The apparent success of modern police in minimizing the effects of civil strife in the three Western cities was tentatively attributed to the political circumstances of protesting and policing. Had governments been illegitimate, or had they adamantly resisted accommodating protest, police policies of restraint probably would not have worked, assuming they had been implemented in the first place. The same general explanation applies to the divergent effects of police reform and expansion on the incidence of common crime. Increased policing can reduce criminal behavior when it reinforces improving socioeconomic conditions. But policing alone cannot counter the corrosive effects of such criminogenic conditions as economic dislocation, social fragmentation, and cultural decay. The "failure" of modern policing to cope with rising levels of disorder is not due to institutional failure but to societal change.

THE FUTURE OF URBAN POLICING

The capacity of the police to maintain public order in the three Western cities probably is more subject to question now than at any time during the past century. Increases in police manpower during the last ten to twenty years have not appreciably slowed rising rates of common crime. Waves of strife during the 1960s and early 1970s appear to have subsided in each city, even in Calcutta, but strife in all the cities has been episodic even in the most turbulent periods. New issues of collective conflict are no doubt in the offing, and some old ones are likely to surface again. We can summarize the factors that most affect present and future policing in these cities under two rubrics: organizational response and social support.

New Responses to Disorder

The prevailing response to crises of public order is "more of the same": more police, more intensive patrolling, improved equipment, and so forth. At some point, however, more substantial and innovative changes are generally attempted.

One such approach is decriminalization. Formally this is a legal response; in practice the police, and courts, are able to selectively criminalize and decriminalize particular kinds of behavior. When serious offenses increase, the police can spare less attention for petty ones. Police organizations also are subject to a variety of formal and informal pressures from other agencies, legislatures, and elite and nonelite interest groups to "tilt" their enforcement activities in one direction or another, or to adapt them in response to shifting judicial policies. The courts, by modifying procedural restraints and by treating particular types of offenses leniently, discourage the policing of certain behaviors and groups. The history of New South Wales is rich in examples of selective police crackdowns (especially on so-called victimless crimes) followed in a few months or years by renewed tolerance. We suggest that the rise in serious disorder is often followed, not by crackdowns, but by police inattention to particularly widespread and nonthreatening offenses. In Sydney, London, and—as far as we know—Calcutta, this kind of adjustment is largely informal. In Stockholm, where there is more insistence on congruence of legal form and police practice, the extensive decriminalization of deviant social behavior, cited previously, reveals a formal shift. We also noted the decriminalization of petty larceny from stores in Sweden. In the other cities police apparently continue to record such offenses, when informed of them, but they evidently lack resources to take effective countermeasures: we showed earlier that reported offenses of this kind have increased far more rapidly in recent years than either arrests or convictions. It may be objected that decriminalization of petty offenses, whether de jure or de facto, is a non-response. On the contrary, it may have the practical positive consequence of freeing scarce police resources for direction toward more serious offenses. Police also may gain in public acceptance if they take a tolerant line to behaviors that are now widespread and, to many, socially tolerable (e.g., abortion, sexual deviance, gambling, loitering, and some kinds of disorderly conduct). Probably more important than either of these factors, though, are the symbolic effects of decriminalization on perceptions of disorder. The public view of crime and deviance involves a good deal of symbolic manipulation and elite persuasion of non-elites about the definition of acceptable behavior. Insofar as crime is created by these symbolic means, it can also be reduced by symbolic means, leaving only that core—no doubt a substantial one—of serious aggressive and acquisitive offenses that are universally abhorred.

There also are more major structural innovations in prospect. The forms created in the nineteenth century police reforms are not necessarily suitable to contemporary circumstances. In Sweden in 1965, for example, the police were nationalized. The immediate stimuli for the reorganization were rising crime rates, a desire for efficiency, and the growing need for directed coordination among diverse local police forces. Two important consequences for policing in Stockholm have been an increase in police size, already remarked, and more effective communication and cooperation between city and suburbs. The English police forces continue to be locally controlled, except for the Metropolitan Police, and nationalization may be in the offing.[8]

The use of private guards and security services is a frequent response to the inability of the police to control property crime. In Sydney, Stockholm, and London, more and more businesses are employing their own guards or obtaining police services on contract from private security agencies. In Stockholm in the early 1970s private police outnumbered public agents, and the government contracted with private institutions to provide guards for foreign embassies. Private police are not new, of course. They are widely used in non-Western societies and, historically, were found in many Western cities. What is exceptional is their rapid expansion now and the possibility that they may have the resources and flexibility to innovate in ways that are closed to public police forces.

Another alternative to public policing is reliance on military and paramilitary organizations, which often are called on to control civil disorder and have been much used in Calcutta throughout the twentieth century. Less frequently, such forces provide more routine police services. They rarely have seen action in twentieth century London, Stockholm, or New South Wales, and when they were used in earlier times in these societies they were the object of intense public hostility, as they are in India today. Any contemporary government that relied on paramilitary police would almost certainly lose a measure of its legitimacy, and such forces surely will not be called on while fear of public disorder in the three Western cities remains at its present level.

Social Support for Policing

That popular police are effective police is an article of liberal faith. Marked differences past and present in the style of policing and in the popularity of the police in the four cities allow us to test this proposition. The London police work individually and unarmed, as they have since 1829, depending heavily for their success on citizen respect and cooperation. Support had to be earned in an atmosphere of public hostility that was particularly intense in the 1830s and again in the 1860s, but an official opinion poll in the early 1960s showed that the English police were generally perceived as they wish to be seen: honest, helpful, and trustworthy.[9] In the last decade, however, the hostility of many youthful activists as well as a sizable segment of the London press, combined with widely publicized instances of corruption, has made a dent in that image.

The police of Stockholm had more difficulty than their London colleagues in living down an unsavory nineteenth century reputation. Riots against police, especially in reaction to arrests, were common for some decades after 1850; the incidence of individual offenses against officials (mainly assaults on police) increased from the 1850s until after 1910. Some of this hostility was no doubt due to the role of police in controlling working-class protest between the 1880s and 1920. In the last 50 years, however, there has been a fundamental change in Stockholmers' attitudes toward the police. Recruiting standards are high, police are well trained and well-paid (equivalent to secondary school teachers), and accusations of corruption or brutality are virtually nonexistent. Recent opinion polls supply convincing evidence of strong public support, though youths in Sweden, as elsewhere, are more hostile toward the police than are other groups.

The police of New South Wales were also unpopular in the nineteenth century, but they seem to have been less actively disliked than members of Stockholm's force. They have had relatively broad functions and considerable discretion in applying the law—more, that is, than the police of London and Stockholm. Since the 1890s they have been armed, and from World War I until 1949 they also had counterespionage and surveillance responsibilities. Moreover police are still recruited largely from the working class, and salaries remain relatively low. The net effect of these factors is that the New South Wales police have never enjoyed a high degree of support. Public suspicion and hostility is apparent in accusations that police are sometimes corrupt, use "basher tactics," and are indiscriminate in making arrests. Polls in the 1960s gave evidence of mixed and declining public support for the force.

There are no opinion polls about police in Calcutta, but it was noted earlier that the common policeman was generally deficient in training and rectitude, underpaid, and unrespected, throughout the years of colonial rule. The continued use of these agents to control strikes and demonstrations is unlikely to have won much public support for the force in recent decades. The police also lacked official support during the years of leftist United Front government in the late 1960s. Like many another group with a grievance in Calcutta, some of them protested in 1971 by rioting at the police superintendent's office and in the state assembly.

High levels of public support for the police in London and Stockholm have had no discernible dampening effect on instances of public disorder in either city. Indeed, public respect for the police in those cities may have encouraged victims of crime to report such incidents to the police, thereby increasing one indicator of public disorder. In New South Wales the rise in crime indicators has been less pronounced, though the police are less popular there—not necessarily by coincidence. In general we have little support for the view that police popularity per se has much to do with keeping crime down. It is certain only that being a policeman, and dealing with one, is somewhat better in London and Stockholm than in Sydney, and much better there than in Calcutta. For the future, two positive consequences may depend on popular respect for the police: Ordinary people may be patient longer with rising disorder, and they may be more likely to accept innovative responses to it—if and when they are devised.

NOTES TO PART II, CHAPTER 4

1. David H. Bayley, "The Police and Political Development in Europe," in Charles Tilly, ed., *The Formation of National States in Western Europe* (Princeton, N.J.: Princeton University Press, 1975), pp. 328-379. Bayley's generalizations are based on a study of the national development of the English, French, German, and Italian police.

2. The history of uniformed policing in the United States begins in 1853, when the New York City police were reorganized on the model of London's Metropolitan Police: see James F. Richardson, *The New York Police: Colonial Times to 1901* (New York: Oxford University Press, 1970). In the next 40 years virtually every one of the 100 largest cities in the United States followed suit, the most populous cities first; see Eric H. Monkkonen, "The Uniformed Police: A Dispersion Model" (unpublished paper, Department of History, University of North Carolina, Charlotte, 1976).

3. A study emphasizing the importance of the middle classes' quest for order as a source of professionalization of the police is Allan Silver, "The Demand for Order in Civil Society: A Review of Some Themes in the History of Urban Crime, Police, and Riot," in David J. Bordua, ed., *The Police: Six Sociological Essays* (New York: Wiley, 1967).

4. Bayley, op. cit., p. 357, argues that since domestic turmoil in England had largely subsided by 1820, disorder played little role in the establishment of the Metropolitan Police. This interpretation seems to ignore the widespread fears of strife voiced by the English elite during the 1820s and the elite's great concern about crimes of violence and theft, reflected in high and rising rates of committals to trial and convictions for these offenses. Moreover the 1839 act requiring all English cities and counties to establish police on the London model was passed at the height of the Chartist movement.

5. There is considerable debate among American historians about the circumstances of police modernization in cities in the United States. Monkonnen, who has reviewed the debate (op. cit.), shows that the timing of modernization depended primarily on the size of cities and, implicitly, on the need for rationalized and efficient urban services. Neither ecological factors such as ethnic composition and industrial base nor episodic ones like rioting had any significant role. But this evidence bears on the diffusion of the police idea in a single society. We want to determine what circumstances led to the introduction of modern police organization in the metropolises of societies that had not previously used it.

6. On the intensification of class conflict in England in these years, see Standish Meacham, "The Sense of an Impending Clash: English Working-Class Unrest Before the First World War," *American Historical Review*, 77 (December 1972). Some of the concurrent increase in police strength had a more prosaic purpose: It was made necessary by the decision to give policemen one free day a week rather than one per fortnight. But this required only 1,600 new men, whereas the force was expanded by about 4,100.

7. A broader but more impressionistic study has come to very similar conclusions about the impact of police professionalization on property crime in nineteenth century Canada, the United States, England, and France: The short-

run effect usually was a recorded increase, the long-run effect usually was a decline. See Charles Tilly, Allen Levett, A. Q. Lodhi, and Frank Munger, "How Policing Affected the Visibility of Crime in Nineteenth-Century Europe and America," in Theodore Ferdinand, ed., *The Criminal Justice System* (forthcoming).

8. There have been successive amalgamations of the English police forces, which (including Wales) numbered 49 as of 1966; roughly half their financial support has been provided by the national government, which uses the power of the purse to ensure uniform practices. Greater efficiency of police work nonetheless might follow from formal nationalization. See T. A. Critchley, *A History of Police in England and Wales, 1900-1966* (London: Constable, 1967).

9. Royal Commission on the Police, *Final Report* (London: Her Majesty's Stationery Office, 1962).

Chapter 5

TRIALS, PUNISHMENT, AND ALTERNATIVES

The fate of those charged with criminal offenses has varied remarkably depending on the time and place. In the eighteenth and early nineteenth centuries a good many people were sentenced to hang for offenses that in some of the four societies would now bring a fine, on evidence that would now result in acquittal. This chapter surveys some of the reforms in courts and court procedure, criminal sanctions, and correctional practices that have contributed to a fundamental change in the consequences of crime for most of those accused of it.

The evolution of punishment in Western societies was much influenced by class and economic considerations.[1] Class interests and cost efficiency are implicated in a good many of the changes reviewed below, but these factors operate in the context of a more fundamental transformation in social values and beliefs about crime and punishment that began in the eighteenth century and is still in train. This is no place for a history of Western social thought, but two changes are strikingly apparent in any review of evolving policies of "law and order" during the last two centuries. One is the decline of brutal and inhumane treatment of offenders, the other is the rise of the belief that crime has mainly social origins, therefore calls for rehabilitation as well as or instead of punishment. These humanitarian views are by no means universally held or applied. The institutions of public order of the four societies we studied embody such principles in differing degrees. One theme in the comparisons to follow is the extent to which humanitarian values and practices have supplanted the repressive ones of past centuries; the underlying issue is to determine the kinds of social and political circumstances that have encouraged the implementation of humanitarian policies.

It is fashionable among liberal scholars and reformers to castigate officials in Western societies for their failure to eliminate substantial residues of repressive law, procedure, and punishment that remain in the bodies politic. This kind of critique often assumes, implicitly or explicitly, that consistent application of humanitarian principles would lead to improved public order. We make no such a priori assumptions. We prefer humanitarian policies, but we think it is an open question whether such policies do in fact reduce threatening social behavior. The evidence to be surveyed may suggest partial answers.

One other initial qualification is needed. The criminal justice system is widely assumed to be the keystone of social defense against individual crime, but in the times and places we studied it has had only an adjunct role in maintaining civil peace. Response to strife has been first of all a political, police, and military matter. The courts and penal institutions have played a significant role in relation to strife only when and where there were political decisions (usually embodied in laws designed to control collective behavior) that rioters, protesters, and revolutionaries be charged, judged, and sentenced like ordinary criminals.

JUDICIAL SYSTEMS

Western systems of defense against crime depend on the courts because they decide the crucial questions of guilt and punishment for almost all major offenses and many petty ones as well. In most medieval societies they were the only regularly constituted institutions of public order; those who arrested offenders and imposed penalties were for the most part agents of the courts. The development of specialized institutions for policing, punishment, and rehabilitation has meant that some quasi-judicial functions are performed elsewhere; for minor offenses, arrest may be tantamount to conviction, and parole boards have much discretion to vary sentences. But the critical decisions for most people accused of crimes are made in court.

Despite their central role in maintaining public order, the courts have rarely been the object of intense controversy or politically motivated reform in the four societies we studied. Crises of public order have seldom been blamed on sins of commission or omission by the courts, as in the United States today, and rarely have led to substantial reform in judicial structure or procedure. The judicial systems of these four societies have been changed fairly often, and there has been a marked expansion in the rights accorded defendants before the courts; but most of these developments have been evolutionary and have occasioned little political debate. There is no paradox here. The judicial function seems to have virtually universal acceptance in Western political theory and practice. From time to time, there have been controversies over which people are brought to court by whom and for what offenses, and over the standards and sanctions to be applied. As a consequence, most efforts and reform in the three Western societies, and even in Bengal, have been directed at the criminal law, policing, and treatment, but not at the existence of the courts or their jurisdication.

The Structure and Jurisdiction of Criminal Courts

The contemporary criminal courts of the four societies have a number of common structural features. All are multitier systems in which petty cases are tried before lesser courts and others are assigned to higher courts according to their nature and seriousness. In the three societies that share the English tradition, the lowest tier is comprised of magistrates' courts. In England the system of magistrates, or justices of the peace, had medieval roots. Traditionally the justices were drawn from the local gentry and unpaid (as they still are in much of the country), and they had responsibility for civil administration as well as summary jurisdiction over a variety of criminal and civil cases. In London in the eighteenth century they had become notoriously venal; reforms in 1792 established a new system of paid (stipendiary) justices having police as well as judicial powers. Magistrates assigned administrative and judicial functions were established in the early years of the New South Wales Colony and in Calcutta in 1793, with further reforms in 1806. In Calcutta these officials supplanted or supplemented a system of East India Company courts in which a mayor's court administered English law and corrupt Indian zamindars administered traditional law for the Indian population. In Stockholm police and judicial responsibilities also were commingled at the lowest level, though not as in London: Petty cases were tried in a police court, which was presided over first by the governor, then by the police commissioner, and after 1864 by a special judge.

In the eighteenth and nineteenth centuries the magistrates' and police courts often exercised jurisdiction over fairly serious (rarely capital) offenses. In the twentieth century, although they deal mainly with petty and administrative offenses, these institutions remain the foundation of the court systems in all four societies. Offenses that carry significant criminal penalties are disposed of by various higher courts. In England the first tier of courts beyond the justices of the peace is the Quarter Sessions, consisting of a number of justices sitting as a panel. The centerpiece of criminal justice in London was and is the Central Criminal Court, a court of assizes whose justices are appointed by the Crown. New South Wales has had a similar three-tier system, but until 1839 its highest court was the Court of Criminal Jurisdiction whose members were military officers; as befitted a penal colony, this was, in effect, a court martial. In Calcutta a Supreme Court established in 1774 was the court of original jurisdiction for all Europeans in Bengal accused of serious crimes, and also for Indians in Calcutta. It applied English common law to European cases and to crimes of violence and theft by Indians. A third, intermediate level of courts was not added until 1957. Stockholm, the smallest city of the four, has the most complex court system. In the nineteenth century it had two courts, later one, for serious offenses, and the High Court of Justice held review powers previously exercised by the king. A major reform in 1942 created the present system, which has three levels beyond the police court. The least serious criminal offenses are tried by a single judge, graver crimes by a three-judge panel, and the weightiest cases by a single professional judge and seven to nine lay judges.

This is sufficient background on the structure of the courts for the comparisons to follow. Note that the dates of court reform given here do not coincide with crises of public order. Of the restructurings just cited, the only one known to have been an issue of public controversy was the 1792 act that reformed the London magistracy, and this was simply one part of a long struggle for legal, judicial, and police reform.

The Rights of Defendants

At least four characteristics of court procedure are important from a defendant's point of view. One involves the question of equity versus discrimination in the court's application of the law. In all the societies the young, the poor, the less-educated, the immigrants, and members of subordinate ethnic groups have been more likely than others to be arrested and committed to trial. But how equitably are they treated once brought before the courts? We managed to gather all too little evidence on this question in the course of so general a study. There are two substantial examples of inequity, though. The case studies provide ample evidence that the courts gave harsher sentences to convicts and ticket-of-leave holders in early nineteenth-century New South Wales, and to Indians in Calcutta during colonial rule, than to other defendants.

The traditional English means of ensuring a fair trial was to permit the accused to be judged by a jury of his peers. However the principle was not immediately extended to New South Wales; jury trials were not used until 1833, and military courts were not abolished until the end of transportation seven years later. Europeans accused of crimes in Calcutta had the right to trial by European juries; Indians lacked a comparable right. There was no such Scandinavian tradition, but a functional equivalent exists in the contemporary Swedish use of panels of judges to decide serious cases. The same kind of principle is evident in the use of panels of justices in Quarter Sessions in both England and New South Wales. The person accused before these courts is not being judged by his peers, but decisions made by a panel of judges presumably moderate the effects of individual judicial bias.

Another mechanism for checking the arbitrariness of individual justices is the right of appeal. Stockholm had an appeals court at least as early as 1614, and it was traditional for the monarch to review all death sentences. In the other three societies death sentences also were subject to review, not always systematically, and often they were commuted. Provisions for appeal of other kinds of sentences were slow to be institutionalized, however. England had limited provision for appeals in 1873, but the first formal criminal appeals court was not established until 1907. New South Wales followed suit in this as in so many other innovations by establishing a Court of Criminal Appeals in 1912. Since 1957 the High Court in Calcutta has served almost exclusively as an appeals court, though it had exercised that function for some time previously. The evidence we have suggests that appeals are not particularly common in any of these societies now, and the decisions of lower courts usually are sustained.

Jury trials and appeal courts aside, the last decades of the nineteenth century saw a general and growing tendency to strengthen the rights of defendants. Some of the steps were procedural. In England the rules of evidence were revised, for example, by permitting the accused to examine witnesses and to testify in his own defense. Similar rights were accorded New South Welshmen in 1891. In India an act of 1872 prohibited the use of confessions to police as evidence in court—a reform whose importance was due to the police practice of coercing confessions. The Swedes have been particularly insistent that courts' decisions take account of the individual's circumstances and characteristics, and since 1964 detailed presentencing investigations have been required.

These reforms theoretically have benefited all defendants. The provision of free legal services to the poor was another thrust of reform having great practical impact, and the Swedes were pioneers. The city of Stockholm paid a lawyer to assist poor defendants beginning in 1884 and in 1913 established a bureau to offer the same services. An act of 1919 made free legal services generally available, at the courts' discretion. At first these services were furnished mainly in civil cases, but after 1919 in a number of defendants in criminal cases also were given help. In 1972 Sweden established a comprehensive system of legal aid in criminal, civil, and administrative cases in which receipt of assistance was a function not of judicial discretion but of the individual's ability to pay.

Despite the repeated urgings of reformers, England and New South Wales made legal services available slowly and grudgingly. Judges were empowered to support the defense of persons on trial for indictable offenses beginning in 1903 in England and in 1907 in New South Wales. In both places political sentiment has consistently opposed the establishment of a public defender's office, though it has been more than 50 years since the first legislative proposals in this regard were tabled. Piecemeal reforms have extended aid to defendants before the magistrates' courts, beginning in England in the 1930s, but use of such assistance continues to be constrained in both law and practice. In New South Wales an act that extended legal aid in 1969 excluded repeat offenders. The most recent English enactments (1964, 1974) require a means test, and it has been estimated that in the early 1970s only five percent of defendants were represented in their first appearance before magistrates' courts. Private agencies have provided some legal services in both countries. In New South Wales, for example, a special legal service was established for aborigines in 1970. Only in Calcutta do we lack evidence of special provisions for legal services for the poor. But in Calcutta almost everyone is poor, and the municipal treasury has no funds even for water and sewerage services; in such circumstances legal aid is neither relevant nor possible.

These illustrative instances of reforms that have improved a defendant's chances of a fair trial in the three Western societies, are more than sufficient to document a substantial trend. Defendants are much more likely now than a century ago to get a full hearing and to have their cases decided consistently and with attention to personal circumstances. It cannot be said that defendants are equals before the courts, but their status has improved greatly and their rights have been expanded. Considerations of economy and efficiency are a hindrance to any broad expansion, though. Legal aid and presentencing investigations are costly, adversarial proceedings in court are time-consuming, and appeals add considerably to the work load of the courts and their administrative agencies.

The increase in defendants' rights, combined with the rising numbers of arrests and committals to trial in the Western cities, are forces quite capable of overloading the criminal justice systems there. Plea bargaining is a popular North American response to such pressures; accused and accuser are partners to a pact in which the judicial system gains efficiency by reducing the defendant's risks and penalties. Plea bargaining is increasingly common in New South Wales but is virtually unknown in Sweden. In England plea bargaining per se is not practiced, but the same purpose is served by allowing the defendant in most criminal cases to opt for a summary trial before a magistrates' court rather than a jury trial before a higher court. Summary justice is speedier, and conviction is probably more certain; but most important for the defendants, the sentences magistrates can impose are limited in severity. The prosecution can give this option to the accused for all but the most serious crimes, and as a consequence about 90 percent of all cases legally triable by higher courts are now heard by magistrates. The system naturally invites comparison with plea bargaining in the United States. The English practice originated in the middle of the nineteenth century, when crime rates were declining, and it has always had explicit legal sanction and ground rules. Plea bargaining in North America has developed as an ad hoc administrative response to the increased number of cases; it has no formal legal basis, nor is it applied consistently.

Alternatives

Plea bargaining and summary justice are by no means the only administrative alternatives to full courtroom hearings of criminal cases. A much different approach is the creation of special bodies and procedures for dealing with particular offenses. This is done under two very different sets of circumstances. When public disorder is particularly great, and especially when political strife is prevalent, many societies resort to special tribunals that sentence dissidents to detention or imprisonment without the usual judicial niceties or rights of appeal. These tribunals are speedy and efficient, they need not be concerned about whether defendants are guilty according to criminal law and rules of evidence, and perhaps above all they function in privacy, out of political view. Such practices are alien to the Scandinavian and English temper, but the English nevertheless employed them against Bengali nationalists from the 1920s through the early 1940s. The Indians have continued to rely on such swift, nonpublic procedures for dealing with dissidents after independence; their imposition nationwide in 1975 was an extension of a means often employed at the state level during the previous 25 years.

The more important and humanitarian alternatives to criminal proceedings are based on the emerging belief that certain categories of offenders, and offenses, require special social treatment. Children who committed crimes were treated the same as adult offenders until well into the nineteenth century. In London in the 1840s, for example, persons aged nineteen and younger made up one-third of those committed for trial, while as late as the 1860s and 1870s between five and nine percent of the prisoners in London's notorious

Newgate Gaol were under sixteen, and a few were younger than twelve. Significantly different treatment of children accused of crimes began in the latter half of the nineteenth century and included the establishment of children's courts featuring special, usually private proceedings, a wide range of judicial discretion in disposing of cases, and special custodial care and home casework services. In Sweden local child welfare boards were given responsibility for such cases beginning in 1902. In New South Wales children's courts were established in 1905, in England in 1908. Women have occasionally been accorded special treatment by the law and courts, for example in New South Wales, but not at present as far as we know. Those who are mentally incompetent or ill also have benefited from special legal provisions; one of the significant thrusts of legal reform in twentieth century England has been to ensure that offenders medically judged insane are treated as such.

Certain kinds of offenses are also thought to warrant special social treatment, hence to require noncriminal adjudication. The Swedes have gone further in this direction than the other societies we studied, beginning with a program for interning vagrants in 1885. Local boards, not courts, passed judgment on persons accused of vagrancy and were empowered to commit vagrants to agricultural colonies for up to three years. Beginning in 1916 local temperance boards were given similar powers to take proceedings against alcoholics, who could be interned, for purposes of rehabilitation, for up to four years. The vagrancy boards no longer exist, and the temperance boards have been transformed; but the basic principle that some offensive forms of social conduct are not necessarily "crimes" but may be problems calling for rehabilitation remains a dominant feature of Swedish institutions of public order. Persons subject to quasi-judicial proceedings for such offenses are no more likely than defendants in criminal proceedings to be protected from capricious decisions, but at least they are not labeled and treated as criminals. New South Wales furnishes an instructive contrast: Drunkenness continues to be treated only as a criminal offense, there are no significant public programs for helping chronic offenders, and the political elite and police prefer to keep it that way, because by prevailing antipodean standards public drunkenness is immoral and public immorality is a crime.

THE TREATMENT OF OFFENDERS

The social ritual called criminal justice sorts people according to their degrees of guilt, and societies have evolved extraordinarily diverse ways of dealing with those judged guilty. The handling of criminals has changed more fundamentally, in these four societies and in Western civilization generally, than have the criminal law, the police, the courts, or perhaps all of them together. The long list of punishments includes execution, physical deprivation, and whipping; deportation; confinement in workhouses, prisons, and reformatories; public ridicule, fines, and loss of civil rights. Treatment of criminals also relied on many more "socially useful" practices: forced labor in galleys, penal colonies, farms, and industry; cautions like suspended sentences, parole, and community supervision; and programs of positive rehabilitation involving moral reeducation, counseling, and training. These treatments have been variously implemented, and there has been much disingenuous rationalization of the moral and social benefits of each. The four societies do not provide examples of all the approaches, but they do offer substantial evidence of the emergence of humanitarian practices, their differential distribution, and the kinds of social forces that have impelled and restrained reform.

Preferences and Possibilities for Treatment

The treatment of criminals in a particular time and place depends partly on what is socially preferable, partly on what is socially possible. Social preferences, infinitely diverse in detail, generally can be categorized as punitive and remedial. "Punitive" preferences and policies emphasize punishment of offenders and deterrence of potential offenders. "Remedial" preferences and policies, as we use the term, are those which seek to put criminals to social use—directly by exploiting their labor, or indirectly by resocializing them to become self-sustaining, productive members of society. Preferences of both kinds are expressed by different groups in contemporary and most historical societies, but we find that the same specific policies can satisfy both kinds of preferences, and many of the innovations in treatment of the last century and more have been devised precisely because they have both remedial and punitive effects. At the outset of this chapter we cited a trend away from callous and brutal treatment of offenders and toward humane policies. That trend is not identical or even highly correlated with a shift from punitive to remedial policies. Many policies designed to serve remedial ends have been incalculably cruel, and humanitarian sentiments have informed many punitive policies.

The policies actually used to treat criminals are constrained by the basic socioeconomic requirements and political dynamics of societies. On the economic front, labor scarcity is an incentive to exploit criminals' labor, even to create "criminals" to undertake unpleasant tasks. If labor is not scarce, other kinds of policies are needed, depending on levels of economic productivity. In poor societies it is preferable to rely on capital and corporal punishments, which are cheap. More prosperous conditions make possible more elaborate and expensive treatments, including both long-term imprisonment and rehabilitation. A potent political principle is that influential social groups can be counted on to oppose the use of punitive and inhumane treatments against themselves and those with whom they identify. The upper classes of most societies we know anything about have usually found ways to spare their deviant members the unpleasantness visited on criminals from other classes. The rise in political influence of the middle classes and, later, the working classes in the three Western societies is a dynamic force that underlies the evolution of humane and rehabilitative treatments. These observations do not explain treatment policies, however, because very substantial cultural and intellectual differences in treatment preferences have always existed independently of economic and class considerations. We think that the evidence reviewed below supports the position that humanitarian and rehabilitative ideologies in Western societies have exerted an independent force on the status and treatment of offenders. The most substantial innovations, of course, have come about when ideological preferences for reform have coincided with favorable economic and political circumstances.

Evidence from the four societies covers four kinds of policies and practices of treatment: the use of physical punishment, the labor alternative, the evolution of custodial care, and alternatives to imprisonment. The kinds of preferences reflected in each are discussed, and where evidence permits we comment on the intellectual and social circumstances that have led to the adoption or decline of each kind of policy.

The Passing of Capital and Corporal Punishment

Punishments for crime in eighteenth century European societies were nasty and cheap. Their nastiness was in large part deliberate, being intended first to deter others who might be tempted to crime, second to exact retribution from the guilty. Capital and corporal sanctions, the first line of social defense for crimes against persons and property, satisfied the prevailing preference for deterrence and punishment. They were not costly to administer, and there were no obvious reasons for thinking them ineffective. Hanging and mutilation were wasteful of manpower, it is true; but where labor was scarce physical punishments could be easily replaced by sentencing offenders to workhouses or transportation.

One measure of the brutality of punishment in the eighteenth and early nineteenth centuries was the frequency with which the death penalty was invoked. Execution was legally prescribed for a great many offenses, including petty ones, and judges had little discretion about whether to apply this penalty to people judged guilty. A seventeenth century writer reports, with reliability that is difficult to establish, that 72,000 thieves were hanged during the reign of the Tudor King Henry VIII, and that during Elizabeth's reign vagabonds were sometimes hanged by the hundreds.[2] But great opposition developed to executions on such a broad scale, not only by those who felt the noose at their neck but by intellectuals and many of the elite and middle classes. The elite in the eighteenth century tended to believe that the threat of capital punishment was necessary to deter crime; but little satisfaction was taken in the imposition of such sentences, and an increasing proportion of them were commuted. There was a growing liberal belief, first loudly voiced by European scholars in the seventeenth century, that capital punishment was needlessly cruel and socially useless, and by the 1780s this view had been incorporated into the new criminal codes of several continental states, where the death penalty was abolished. The declining incidence of capital punishment in England, Sweden, and New South Wales is represented in Figure II.1.5, which indicates that by 1850 this sanction was rarely used.[3] Since the data are not weighted for population, they substantially understate the rate of decline. But it should also be noted that the crises of public order in the 1830s and 1840s are reflected in temporary increases in executions. The argu-

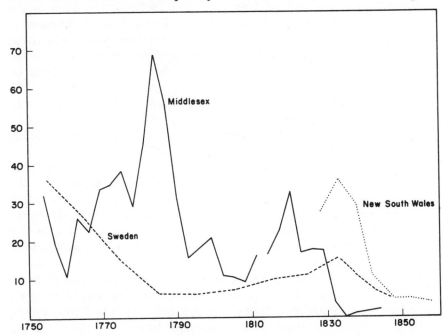

Figure II.5.1 Average annual executions in Middlesex, Sweden, and New South Wales, 1750-1860

ments against capital punishment were not enough to dissuade officials under stress from stepping up reliance on the older methods.

One alternative to capital punishment was corporal punishment. Like executions it usually was administered publicly, both for its general deterrent effect and to contribute to the social embarrassment of the offender. Its use also declined in the nineteenth century, and by 1900 it had virtually disappeared as a judicially prescribed penalty in the three Western societies. Corporal punishment was regularly used to maintain prison discipline long after it had passed from public view, however. In Sweden and England whippings and other physical punishments were rarely imposed by the courts after the mid-nineteenth century. In Sweden they were not formally prohibited in prisons until 1925. In England the use of corporal punishment for disciplinary infractions in prisons was not abandoned until 1963. In New South Wales flogging and other physical punishments were used unstintingly during the convict era. Legislation passed in 1830, for example, prescribed up to twelve months hard labor in chains, or 100 lashes, for convicts convicted of drunkenness, neglect of work, or use of abusive language. The judicial bite was as sharp as its bark: In the mid-1830s 6,000 to 7,000 floggings a year were administered by the courts to a convict population of no more than 30,000. Corporal punishment was resorted to much less frequently after the end of transportation in 1840, but even in the 1890s there are police records of men being flogged in cases of wanton assault. Such physical punishments as bread-and-water diets, gagging, and floggings continued in official use in prisons until the turn of the century. The New South Wales tradition of relying on such chastisements was symbolically alive until very recently. A 1929 act broadened the circumstances under which judges could prescribe whipping, and a judge publicly urged a return to the practice in 1946. In fact the legal provisions have almost never been invoked in this century and were abolished by law in 1974.

Authorities in Bengal still rely on corporal punishment, as far as we know, but with the same diminution evident in Europe. Capital punishment has not been outlawed, but we lack recent information on the frequency of executions. Whippings were generously meted out by the courts not only in the nineteenth century but also in response to the early twentieth century episodes of Bengali nationalism. Prison reports from nineteenth century jails show extensive use of handcuffs and leg irons, whipping, and deprivation of food; and cases continued to occur, though less and less frequently through the 1950s and 1960s. During colonial rule Europeans in Bengal prisons received such treatment less often than did Indians, however.

The Labor Alternative

Capital and corporal punishment did no more than deter and punish. The alternative of putting criminals to work has an equally long European heritage, but the rationales vary from the exploitation of criminals' labor for public or private profit to the teaching to criminals of skills and habits they could profitably employ on release. A third rationale was punishment, by forcing prisoners to do work more rigorous and painful than they would voluntarily accept. Offenders were given many different tasks, depending on economic circumstances and prevailing views about punishment and rehabilitation.

Houses of correction were a common feature of European cities from the early seventeenth century. London's Bridewell was established in 1555, Stockholm's *spinnhuss* in the following century. Their inmates were mainly vagrants, beggars, and petty criminals who did routine work that was expected to turn a profit for the houses' public or private management. The contemporary view of these institutions is well summarized by Rusche and Kirchheimer:

> The essence of the house of correction was that it combined the principles of the poorhouse, workhouse, and penal institution. Its main aim was to make the labor power of unwilling people socially useful. By being forced to work within the institution, the prisoners would form industrious habits and would receive a vocational training at the same time. When released, it was hoped, they would voluntarily swell the labor market.[4]

The late eighteenth and early nineteenth centuries were a time of labor surplus in most European societies, however, and penal institutions run on capitalist principles illustrated in microcosm the Marxian thesis about the effects of declining profits on the immiseration of labor. Conditions for inmates, which in earlier times often had been tolerable by prevailing standards, sank to abysmal levels. In Stockholm some public attention and funds apparently were given to the workhouses during this period, and vagrants were offered the choice of military service.

The English had one attractive alternative to both capital punishment and unprofitable workhouses: transportation of offenders to the colonies, where labor could be put to good use. Transportation was a feature of English penal practice as early as 1597. The American colonies were planted with the help of tens of thousands of convicts, and the Botany Bay colony was founded in direct response to the need to remove the hundreds of prisoners who were stockpiled in convict ships in the River Thames after the American Revolution. By the 1830s the free settlers and emancipists of New South Wales were able to press for the end of transportation; they were successful in 1840, but the practice continued elsewhere in Australia until

1867. All told, an estimated 150,000 English and Irish convicts were transported to Australia. In New South Wales the prisoners were sometimes used for public works but more often were assigned to private employers, individually or in groups, as servants and laborers. Those who were unemployable or particularly dangerous were imprisoned, either in the colony or by secondary transportation to Norfolk Island. Convicts who had served their terms were released, and many remained to swell the colony's labor force. Sweden, lacking colonies to which convicts could be transported, experimented with the assignment of convicts to labor under private supervision. Stockholm maintained such programs through the 1890s.

One rationale for putting offenders to work shifted in the course of the nineteenth century when the economic incentives were undercut. Prisoners were proportionally fewer in the three Western societies as the century progressed, as is evident from the declining conviction rates reviewed previously. Probably more important was the growing capital investment needed to make profitable use of labor in all the societies, coupled with the opposition of private businessmen to cut-rate competition by prison workshops and, later, the objections of organized labor on the same grounds. The rehabilitative purposes remained, but they were best served through training programs rather than forced labor per se. One significant innovation began in London during the 1850s, when a new system of reformatories for child offenders was established. Previously children had been briefly jailed for each offense, then released to resume seeking their livelihood by the only means open to most of them, namely, petty thievery. The youngsters now were committed to reformatories long enough to receive basic education and work training.[5]

The concern for work-as-punishment remained and prompted a number of odious innovations. Prison authorities in England and New South Wales were particularly fond of treadmill labor—regardless of whether the mills' energies were harnessed. A committee in the New South Wales observed, after an investigation in 1825, that treadmill labor was a very effective punishment by virtue of its monotonous and irksome regularity and concluded "that if coercive labour and restraint is calculated to reform or deter from crime, no system of discipline can better be calculated for this purpose than that of the tread-wheel. . . ."[6] Prisons in most Western societies continued to require labor of some convicts in the twentieth century, but rarely was the rationale so punitive. The primary justification is rehabilitation; profitable productivity is secondary, and convicts in the three Western societies receive at least token payment for their work.

We have no evidence that prison labor was widely used or rationalized in Bengal in the period we studied.

Prison Reform and Custodial Care

The lessening reliance on physical punishment, the declining profitability of workhouses, the dramatic increase in crime and convictions in the 1820s and 1830s, and, in England, the restriction of transportation in the 1840s made it essential to devise different methods for treating offenders. The principal thrust of innovation in the three Western societies was prison expansion and reform. At least two different strands can be seen in the skein of reform. The same liberal sensitivities that championed reduction of capital and corporal punishment were aroused by the horrors of prison existence. Prisons in the late eighteenth century included the houses of correction, workhouses—which warehoused a motley crew of social undesirables, among them debtors, the insane, and petty criminals—and jails, which temporarily incarcerated people awaiting trial and execution of sentence for a great variety of offenses. These institutions typically housed without segregation people of all ages, both sexes, and every social category in ancient, cramped, unsanitary quarters. The inmates were ill-fed, their labor was exploited, and their money—if they had any—was extracted as fees by the goalers. John Howard, an English prison official of the 1770s, began what became an international movement for the reform of such conditions. The objects were to relieve the misery of prisoners and to improve their chances of rehabilitation.

The second strand of reformist thought was concerned less with implementing humanitarian principles than with establishing rational and efficient systems of custodial punishment. Criminals were to be sentenced to convict prisons in proportion to the seriousness of their offenses, and there was to be regular discipline, including especially the discipline of hard labor, both as punishment and as a source of moral regeneration.

The pace and substance of prison reform varied considerably from country to country. In Sweden efforts at improving prison conditions and treatment were inspired in part by John Howard's international movement and date from the 1780s. The effective impetus for prison reform came in 1840, and it came from the top down. In 1840 Crown Prince Oscar wrote a treatise *On Punishments and Prisons*, reflecting the most advanced thinking of the time. After he became king in 1844 Oscar encouraged the rapid introduction of a wide range of reforms in which the rehabilitation of the prisoner and his reintegration into society were the primary goals. Thirteen new

prisons were built by 1850, 34 by 1864, and placed under coordinated national management; prisoners were classified and assigned to
specialized institutions according to their offenses and prospects for
rehabilitation, and programs of vocational and religious training were
introduced. Citizens' aftercare societies, modeled on those of London and Philadelphia, were promoted with an eye to smoothing
ex-convicts' return to society. This early and programmatic start on
penal reform was followed by successive innovations that have continued to the present. Minimum-security institutions were established
late in the nineteenth century, and judges were given wide latitude in
sentencing by the 1865 criminal code. In this century a variety of
alternatives to imprisonment have been implemented. The most
recent (1974) reform in imprisonment per se guarantees rights to
inmates, including some form of participation in prison decision
making.

Prison reform in England was more gradual. Acts in 1823 and
1835 implemented some of the reformers' long-standing pleas for
more humane treatment in prisons, and houses of correction and
prisons came to be supported from public funds and inspected by
officials. Debtors' prisons were abolished in the 1840s as nonpenal
methods for dealing with these offenders were devised. The pressures
of a growing convict population inspired a spate of prison building
from the 1820s to the 1850s. In the 1830s and 1840s there was also
considerable experimentation with the "silent system," in which
prisoners were kept in isolation, forbidden to speak, and sometimes
prevented from seeing other prisoners, so that they could contem-
plate their sins in privacy and undergo a natural moral rejuvenation.
The reformers' good intentions foundered on two hard facts: such
systems were expensive, and the inmates, rather than finding inner
moral strength, all too often went mad. But nothing resembling a
comprehensive national program of treatment was designed until the
1853 Penal Servitude Act, which provided for hard and presumably
rehabilitative labor in convict prisons for men who before that date
would have been transported to Australia. English prisons were
centralized under Home Office control in 1877, but for the next two
decades the principal result was that imprisonment was made consistently harsh. The rigors of English prisons gradually began to abate
around the turn of the century, and especially during the tenure of
Liberal governments in the decade before World War I. The prison
population was reduced by more than half between 1905 and 1918,
for example, and the Borstal system for offenders aged 16 to 21 was
inaugurated and expanded. In the 1930s and since World War II
diversification has continued, with the development of open facilities
for adult offenders, the use of detention centers as alternatives to

conventional prisons, and creation of many specialized facilities. For the bulk of the prison population, though, the primary emphasis has not greatly changed: Prisons are designed to deter and punish as much as to rehabilitate.

The New South Wales prison system has had a strongly punitive orientation from the beginning. Nonetheless, serious efforts at devising positive programs of rehabilitation were made beginning early in the nineteenth century. During the penal colony days it was customary to grant "tickets of leave" to deserving convicts, but attempts to introduce incentive systems for well-behaved and productive prisoners were suppressed by higher authority when attempted in 1810-1820, the early 1840s, and again in the 1850s. A select committee in 1861 advocated substantial reforms, but few were made. In the 1880s and 1890s the prisons were overcrowded by drunks, vagrants, the aged, and the insane, and little money or attention was given to rehabilitation. The first wide-ranging prison reforms, introduced in the mid-1890s, included classification and assignment of prisoners according to type of offense, improvement of libraries, remission of sentences, probation for first offenders, and the establishment of associations for aiding discharged prisoners—much the same kinds of practices that had been initiated in Sweden some 50 years earlier.

The timing of the New South Wales reforms bears some explanation. Early reforms in Sweden had royal backing, and the initial English reforms were the result of a century of advocacy by liberal members of the middle class. The main impetus for prison reform and policies of rehabilitation in New South Wales has come from the working class—and organized labor did not gain substantial political influence until the turn of the century. Since then reforms have been slow and have met resistance from conservative, mainly middle-class and rural political groups. In 1905 provisions were made for indeterminate sentences (i.e., terms that could be varied according to the rehabilitative progress of the defendant), but this type of sentencing was rarely used because it challenged the dominant preference for punishment. Special facilities for juveniles were established as early as the 1880s, but the first minimum-security facilities for adult offenders were set up only in the late 1920s. Reforms since World War II have included better classification systems, the introduction of psychological counseling services, and in 1951 an institutionalized parole system—long after such systems were established in most of the West.

"Reform" seems to be inappropriate to describe what has happened in the prisons of Bengal during the past century, although there is some evidence of relative improvement. Prison sentences in

Bengal in the nineteenth and twentieth centuries were usually rather short, from a few months to a few years. An economic motive can be inferred: Prison costs are reduced by keeping sentences brief. Imprisonment had its risks, however. A prison report for 1852-1853 notes that the inmates of the Presidency Jail in Calcutta had a mortality rate of some thirteen percent per year (cf. two percent in English jails of the period); this was attributed to bad diet, unsanitary prison conditions, and the "poor health" of new prisoners. By the turn of the century prison mortality was down to perhaps six percent a year. Colonial commissions and officials sometimes recommended improvements in the jails, but the suggestions were generally rejected, one ground being that the institutions might become too attractive to impoverished Bengalis. In the twentieth century, and especially since independence, prison reports reflect an ideological commitment to rehabilitation; scarce resources presumably prevent the implementation of broadly effective policies. The practical penal "reform" in Bengal is this: From the 1920s on there has been a decline in the average length of sentence, and since independence fewer offenders have been committed to prison. The moral is clear enough. Custodial care and rehabilitation in a prison setting are a social luxury that poor societies now can afford no more easily than could their European counterparts three centuries ago.

Imprisonment became the principal means of punishment for serious crime in all three Western societies during an era when conviction rates were declining. At the dawn of the present century, prisons in England and New South Wales were grim places, and those of Sweden were only slightly less unpleasant. The existence and reputation of these institutions may have had a general deterrent effect for people outside them; their inmates certainly were kept out of circulation and mischief for longer periods than at present. Objectively, reforms have made prison existence less uncomfortable. Subjectively, however, prisons impose a loss of freedom and comfort that probably are as severe, by comparison with contemporary standards of life outside prison, as they were a century ago. If prisons now have lost their presumed deterrent effects, it is not because of their "comforts." The rapid increase in convictions during the last 25 years has far outpaced prison expansion, which means that fewer people can be sent to prison, and sentences are shorter. These constraints on officials fit hand in glove with reformers' urgings that more reliance be placed on noncustodial treatment. For officials, the immediate costs of noncustodial alternatives are lower. And from the point of view of the offender, the risks of prison are thereby reduced. The ultimate social costs of this calculus depend on the alternatives to punishment and their effects.

Alternatives to Imprisonment

One ancient alternative to imprisonment is the imposition of fines. Throughout the era dealt with in this study, offenders could pay fines in lieu of nastier punishments, especially for petty offenses but also for some more serious ones. The use of fines introduces a specific kind of class bias into punishment; those who are prosperous can pay their way out of trouble, and the poor (like debtors previously) are subject to imprisonment. In the three Western societies various reforms have been made to reduce this kind of inequity. In England, after 1914 when a law was passed giving individuals additional time to pay fines, prison admissions in default of fines declined by half. In 1972 a system of "community service orders" was inaugurated: Offenders could be required to give their free time to community projects in lieu of fines or imprisonment. In New South Wales, where many were imprisoned for nonpayment of fines, partial payment entitled the offender to partial remission of sentences beginning in 1899. Even so, as of 1919 two-thirds of new prisoners were jailed for default on fines. Sweden has followed the more equitable procedure: Beginning in the 1930s policies were introduced whereby fines are assessed in proportion to offenders' income and can be paid in installments. In Calcutta, in what appears to be a policy of growing leniency, the average fine assessed has declined since the 1920s.

Fines are an alternative to imprisonment but a punishment nevertheless. The most significant innovations of the twentieth century are those designed to encourage the reintegration of offenders into society. One of the earliest and most widespread practices of this kind is the suspended sentence, coupled with probation services: in a phrase, warning and help. In England after 1879, first offenders could be "bound over" (i.e., discharged on payment of security), and a system of supervised probation was introduced in 1907. Since 1972 courts are enjoined from imprisoning defendants who have not been in prison before, unless convinced no other measures are appropriate, and have been empowered to defer sentences for up to six months, then suspend them altogether if circumstances warrant. New South Wales provided probation for first offenders in 1894 and has continued to expand the system. In Sweden judges could award suspended sentences beginning in 1906, first for offenses that called for sentences of up to six months, later (1918) for sentences of up to one year, and now (since 1944) for sentences up to two years. Parole systems serve a similar function for prisoners who have served part of their sentence and are judged ready to return to ordinary life. New South Wales was late in devising regular parole procedures but expanded the new programs rapidly; between 1965 and 1971 the number of prisoners annually released on parole tripled. Sweden introduced regular parole procedures at the same time as probation, and 70 percent of the persons for whom the Corrections Board had responsibility were not in institutions by 1965; in 1975 the figure exceeded 80 percent. These policies work because there is an extensive system of community-based corrections and aftercare. In the mid-1970s Sweden had 12,000 volunteer supervisors of parolees and probationers.

The ultimate thrust of innovation in rehabilitation is to do away with imprisonment entirely. Nothing in the English, New South Wales, or Bengal experience suggests that these countries are on the verge of closing their jails, but Sweden has moved decidedly in that direction. The number of persons in custody in Sweden has declined steadily, and by 1975 they numbered only 4,000 in a population in excess of 8,000,000. About half of those were in minimum-security and youth facilities. The Swedish prisoners benefited from a furlough system, instituted in 1938 and since expanded, whereby about 10,000 home visits a year are granted. In addition there are holiday prisons where long-term prisoners spend time with their families. A number of prisoners also take advantage of a work release program (as they do in England and New South Wales), spending their working days away from prison. Despite this exceptional emphasis on reintegration, the current view is that institutional treatment remains a barrier to rehabilitation and increases recidivism. A number of Swedish officials and academics favor the elimination of custodial care for all but a handful of the most dangerous offenders.

Sweden has been in the forefront of the twentieth century movement toward noncustodial rehabilitation, but the same tendencies are evident to a lesser degree in England, New South Wales, and other Western societies. In 1976, for example, some members of Britain's ruling Labour Party proposed that imprisonment be abolished as a punishment for property crime. We may ask in conclusion what motives and interests underlie the tendency. The basic social purpose is not very different from the humanitarian objectives expressed by John Howard or for that matter by the middle-class nineteenth century advocates of the work ethic. Simply, it is to salvage the lives of offenders so that they can become "normal" and productive members of society. The "radical" innovations of Swedish and other penal reformers are based on the premise that imprisonment is an inhumane and inadequate means to an end that is better achieved by community-based rehabilitation. Like other intellectual currents of reform in policies of public order, this one has not come to fruition by sheer intellectual force. Two practical conditions have reinforced it, one economic and the other political. Prisons are expensive institutions, expecially when prison labor can no longer be exploited to public profit. Resistance to prison expansion evidently was an important consideration for those who established probation systems and partial remission of sentences in New South Wales at the beginning of the century. It also helped motivate the expansion of probation and parole in the three Western societies in the 1960s and 1970s. Given a rising number of convicted offenders, it is cheaper to release the least dangerous individuals than to build new facilities.

The political condition for policies of reform and rehabilitation is provided by the leaders and legislative spokesmen of labor parties, who usually have been more ready than middle-class parties in all three Western societies to support rehabilitative over punitive policies. The working classes have provided the bulk of the clientele of the prison systems of all societies we know anything about, and in these three societies in particular, working-class leaders are only a few decades removed from the era in which labor activists were often imprisoned. Thus the contemporary penal reforms advocated by liberal and radical experts and officials have an economic rationale that appeals to the more prosperous classes, as well as a natural political base of support. This interpretation—it is only that—is not necessarily applicable to other societies nor to the United States in particular, because evidence suggests that the American working class feels more victimized by crime than by punishment. The future prospect in all the Western societies is that ordinary citizens' growing fear of crime will erode support for policies of leniency and rehabilitation that do not seem to work. The empirical evidence, however, suggests that offenders dealt with leniently are not much more or less likely to show up again in court than those dealt with harshly.[7] The real roots of the problem seem to lie not in recidivism per se but in the growing number of people who indulge in crime in the first place.

NOTES TO PART II, CHAPTER 5

1. See especially Rusche and Kirchheimer, op. cit.

2. Christian Henelius, *Tractatus politicus de Aerario* (Berlin, 1670), p. 325, cited in Rusche and Kirchheimer, op. cit., p. 19.

3. The data are averaged by decade for Sweden, and in five- and three-year intervals for New South Wales and Middlesex, respectively. The sources of the Swedish and New South Wales data are given in our studies of Stockholm and Sydney. The Middlesex data for 1750 to 1810 are from Leon Radzinowicz, *A History of English Criminal Law and its Administration from 1750*, Vol. I (London: Stevens, 1948). After 1811 they are our compilation from *Parliamentary Papers, Accounts and Papers:* 1818 (419) XVI 183; 1819 VIII 4; 1819 (62) XVII 295; 1830-31 (105) XII 461; 1837 (165) XLVI 255; 1842 (36) XXXII 545; 1846 (21) XXXIV 763.

4. Rusche and Kirchheimer, op. cit., p. 42.

5. See J. J. Tobias, *Crime and Industrial Society in the Nineteenth Century* (London: Penguin, 1972), pp. 88-107, 249-252.

6. New South Wales Legislative Council, "Extracts from the Report of the Committee on the Subject of Tread-Wheel Labour" (Sydney: 1825), p. 348.

7. Comparative evidence on recidivism was not gathered in this study. The empirical evidence up to the 1960s has been summarized in a series of reports prepared for the Council of Europe, e.g. Leslie T. Wilkins, *The Effectiveness of Punishment and Other Measures of Treatment for Adult Offenders* (Strasbourg: Council of Europe, Criminological Research Council, 1965, mimeo).

Chapter 6

TOWARD A THEORY OF
PUBLIC DISORDER

Thus far this study has hewed close to the historical facts of crime, civil strife, and the political context of such activities in four urban societies. The evidence has sometimes suggested interpretations and generalizations that challenge conventional wisdom, but always with the implicit qualification that they are based on less-than-complete information from a less-than-representative sample of societies. This chapter moves beyond the particulars of London, Stockholm, Sydney, and Calcutta to a more general understanding of the conditions on which public order and disorder depend. This effort takes the form of a theoretical model, not a formal theory. It specifies the kinds of conditions that cause disorder and maps their connections, but does not include the definitions and hypotheses required by fully elaborated theory. It draws upon the evidence of the four city studies to illustrate these causal connections, but does not claim that the evidence is a test of the model. The model came first, in the sense that the core of it was specified before the city studies were carried out. It was then a heuristic device, a guide to collecting and ordering information on a disorderly subject. Now there is sufficient information to amplify it, and we hope that others will find it worth using and testing.

THEORIES OF CRIME AND CONFLICT

Public disorder consists of threatening collective and individual actions that are subject to public control; the definition was elaborated in Chapter I.2. A general explanation or theory of public disorder as defined here should stipulate the conditions under which diverse kinds of social disorder become a matter of public concern, what kinds of interests and circumstances determine the shape of public response, and the effects of public control on disorder—as well as the impact of disorder on public policies. We know of no such theoretical explanation. Changes in the extent of social disorder obviously are one major source of change in public disorder, even though there is no one-to-one correspondence between the two. The etiology of social disorder therefore provides a well-explored point of departure for a theory of public disorder.

Criminogenic Theories

Studies that offer explanations of "crime"[1] address three rather different questions. First, what "causes" individuals to commit criminal acts? This is usually answered by citing some combination of the physical and mental characteristics of the offender and of his social experience and circumstances. Second, what determines whether an individual is labeled and treated as a criminal? The typical answer refers to the characteristics and interests of the enforcers. Third, why do the extent and type of criminal behaviors differ from one social group to another and from one time to the next?

The third question is more relevant to the determination of the causes of changes in public disorder, but most answers given draw on elements of the explanations offered in response to the first two questions. "Crime" is greater in some places and times because there and then are concentrated certain types of people. Or social conditions conspire there to generate frequent criminal behavior. Or at these junctures the enforcers are most interested in asserting their control.

There are numerous criminogenic theories in each category described, but none is universely accepted, and most are used by scholars and officials alike in eclectic combination with other theories. This tendency to devise multiple and ad hoc explanations for "crime" is reinforced by the great variety of "criminal" behaviors. Some explanations fit some kinds of threatening behavior better than others. Nettler has reviewed many current criminogenic theories that cite social factors and classifies them into four types.[2] Two focus on some form of culture conflict: The source of "crime" is said to be "some division within a society that is associated with differential acceptance of legal norms." Subcultural explanations attribute "crime" to the distinctive standards of behavior said to characterize lower class and ethnic groups; some of the "normal" behaviors of these groups are so deviant from the standards of dominant groups that they are labeled and treated as criminal. Structural explanations attribute "crime" to disparities between peoples' socially induced wants and the means available for their satisfaction; people whose social means are painful to use, limited, or ineffective are likely to resort to criminally deviant ways of getting what they want.[3] The two kinds of theory are not necessarily inconsistent. Entire social groups may be "structurally" handicapped in the pursuit of goals that other groups enjoy freely, and in response the former may develop deviant "subcultural" means to achieve satisfaction.

The other two kinds of explanation Nettler labels "sociopsychological." They "place more of the causal emphasis upon the individual actor, or upon 'kinds' of actors, and upon the interaction between these persons." Symbolic-interactionist theories attribute criminal behavior to what people learn from others about the relative desirability of different ways of acting, and how they learn to think of themselves from what others label them and do to them.[4] Control theories do not ask why people engage in criminal behavior, but why most people most of the time remain within the law. The answer in these theories is "discipline," both that which is internalized by children during socialization and that which is imposed by external social pressure and authorities later in life.[5] These two kinds of theory also are mutually compatible, at least at a very general level. People will do what they are encouraged to do and control what they are obliged to control; but if others' demands on them are too painful, they may react by living up to parents' and authorities' worst rather than best expectations.

The cultural conflict and sociopsychological approaches to explaining "crime" have enough common ground to justify joining them in a kind of universal social theory. Such a theory is likely to be too abstract to be tested or to inform policy, however. By attempting to explain everything in general, it would risk explaining nothing in particular. Moreover such a theory would be difficult if not impossible to assess in most kinds of historical and comparative research. Historical studies of crime and public order are limited to what can be observed mainly in records of public (especially official) policies and actions, and to aggregate measures of demographic and economic conditions. Information on the beliefs, social wants, and opportunities of less-advantaged historical groups is scanty. The same is true of information on such matters as how and how well or badly children have been socialized. What the sociological theorist should be testing—namely, the effects of cultural conflict and lacunae in social control on the extent of deviant or disorderly behavior—the historian will be disposed to treat as an assumption: Changes in criminality are visible evidence of shifting patterns of cultural conflict and social control that can best be detected by observing their consequences for public order.

The principal limitation of the sociological explanations of crime just reviewed is their inattention to crime's political circumstances. When political factors are weighed in, as in labeling theory, or in Richard Quinney's work, it generally is in the form of simplistic assumptions about the self-serving or class-serving operation of structures of authority. Political interests and institutions are a good deal more diverse, and have more variable effects on crime and public order, than is suggested by the criminogenic theories already surveyed. Some of these political conditions are incorporated in the preliminary theory of public disorder to be proposed. First, however, we review some of the explanations put forward for the other face of social disorder, civil strife.

The Etiology of Civil Strife

General theories about civil strife tend to concentrate on one of two areas. The first kind of theorizing considers why and how particular kinds of conflict occur. Revolution is the most popular subject here; coups d'état also have attracted a good deal of theoretical attention and so have riots, especially ethnic and communal riots. The second area involves the factors that determine the types and magnitude of civil strife in entire societies. The first kind of theory is concerned with a class of events, the second with the common properties of many kinds of events. Yet the two are complementary, the second kind of theory being the more general.

There are at least four distinguishable approaches to explaining civil strife, in particular forms or in general. Two share a concern with the psychological properties of people who participate in strife, the others explain strife solely in terms of properties of social systems. To give them labels, they are psychological, sociopsychological, social structural, and group conflict theories, respectively. In attempting to account for the behavior of participants in strife, some psychological theories specify the psychodynamic processes that make revolutionary leaders, others emphasize the extent to which rebels share such psychological properties as alienation and frustration.[6] The sociopsychological theories begin with premises about the conflict-disposing states of mind of rebels but put the weight of explanation on the social conditions that create or alter those states of mind. Some also specify the situational conditions that determine how men act on their motivations and attitudes. A premise common to a number of these theories is that strife is a collective response to discontent, which arises from discrepancies between peoples' expectations and attainments. To explain strife it therefore is necessary to identify the social conditions that increase men's expectations or frustrate their attempts to obtain satisfaction.[7]

The social-structural theories of strife differ in emphasis rather than kind from the more psychological theories. They assume that a fundamental social dislocation, sometimes called "strain" or "dysfunction," is the necessary precondition for strife. The origins of social dislocation are specified, as are the conditions influencing its outcome. But little or no attention is given to the psychological manifestations.[8]

These approaches to theory all purport to explain why groups resist or challenge the social status quo. A competing paradigm for theory asks, not "why men rebel," but how and why it is that groups in societies come into conflict. The group conflict theories in this tradition all assume that strife arises from competition between groups for valued conditions and positions. Some of them, like Marx's theory of revolutionary change, emphasize the class bases of conflict: They are concerned with contention between top-dog and underdog groups over their respective shares of goods, power, and status. Other group conflict theories attribute strife to differences of interest among groups and institutions generally, not just those bearing a hierarchic relation to one another.[9] The most consequential difference between the two approaches to conflict theory is that the former focuses on a more limited set of instances, namely, those involving repression and resistance.

Theoretical explanations of civil strife, like the criminogenic theories, can be shown to converge at a very abstract level. All assume that strife occurs because people, individually or collectively, are prevented from attaining their objectives by constraints imposed by circumstances—including what other groups have and do. The greater such constraints on a group of people, the more likely its members are to clash with other groups. Such an "explanation" is almost truistic, but it is useful in a theory of public disorder: Some such mechanism can be assumed to determine the extent of civil strife in any society at any time.

THE IMMEDIATE CONDITIONS OF PUBLIC DISORDER

Explaining why "crime" and civil strife occur is not the same as accounting for the extent of public disorder. Only some kinds of threatening behavior are regarded as a public responsibility, and the boundaries between "public" and "private" vary widely. Within the "public" realm some groups are much better able than others to translate their concerns into policies of public control. These two kinds of conditions are of equal and immediate importance in determining the effective scope of public disorder: the laws defining public disorder and the policies and institutions established to translate legal conceptions into practical control. The first delineate the formal boundaries of publicly unacceptable disorder, specify penalties, and in effect provide a warrant for collective action. The latter determine how much effort can in fact be given to detecting, controlling, and punishing those who violate the laws. Attempts at controlling disorder can increase because of a change in patterns of threatening behavior; they also can increase because legal redefinitions direct attention to new kinds of "criminality" and collective behavior. Moreover the extent of crime and strife that is officially recorded and policed has spinoff effects on the perceptions of disorder held by officials and their political public, and their willingness to countenance greater, or different, efforts at control.

To account for changes in public disorder we must understand not only why behavior changes, but why legal definitions and policies of public order are changed. One source of change is growing public concern about disorder: Authorities may formulate new laws and policies to give the appearance of action in response to increasing social disorder, and those laws and policies may ultimately reduce the activities that give rise to public concern. In other words there is a good deal of circularity in the processes that generate public disorder. This argument is summarized in Figure II.6.1, where each

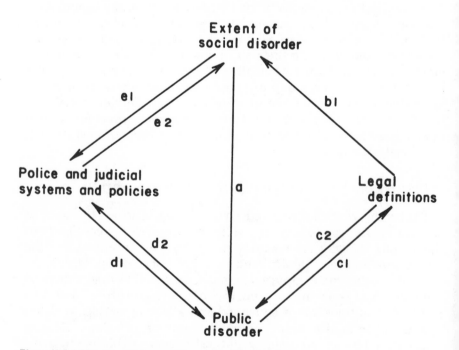

Figure II.6.1 The immediate conditions of public disorder

arrow means "is one of the causes of." Each of the lettered arrows can be described in general terms.

Definitions and Public Disorder (c_1, c_2)

Official definitions of crime vary considerably among societies and over time within them. Rising concern about disorder is one of the principal sources of change in definitions. A simple example of the authoritative redefinition of crime was the New South Wales Masters and Servants Act of 1828, which created the offenses of neglect of work and absence from work. There was presumably little change in real behavior, but authorities decided—during a severe labor shortage—to criminalize, sanction, and thereby reduce a particular kind of undesirable behavior.[10] In this instance elites' concern about disorder had impelled redefinition, a connection symbolized by the arrow c_1. The creation of a new kind of offense, in this example and in general, is usually followed by increased arrests and prosecutions, which all show up in criminal statistics as an upward trend in criminality, a consequence represented by arrow c_2. Thus the broadening of legal definitions ordinarily increases the extent of "public disorder" as measured by indicators of crime.

The interests that motivate expanding concepts of criminality are not necessarily those of a small elite. In Sweden a temperance movement established in the 1870s became one of the great popular movements of Swedish society, mobilizing members of the working class no less than middle-class and professional people. Holding that alcohol was the principal source of misery and poverty among the workers, the movement tried strenuously to restrict the sale of intoxicating beverages by controlling production and distribution and by outright prohibition. Public drunkenness had long been a criminal offense in Stockholm, but the laws enacted in response to the demands of the temperance movement created categories of offenses for those who distilled and distributed corn brandy and sold beer in violation of the new regulations. The rates of crime increased as a consequence. The temperance movement also led, eventually, to the treatment of alcoholism as a social disease rather than a crime.

Concern about civil strife also affects and is affected by legal definitions. When particular kinds of strife become issues of elite or general concern, a typical response is the passage of laws that criminalize some of the behaviors in question. In England in the nineteenth century (and earlier) a great many bills designed to eliminate or restrict what are now called trade unions were drafted especially to give magistrates powers to punish labor organizers and strikers. In Bengal between 1900 and the end of colonial rule there were approximately fifteen major modifications in the criminal law, of which eleven aimed specifically at controlling collective political action—by declaring associations illegal, banning various kinds of public meetings, providing for detention and the suspension of civil rights, and so forth. These laws were widely employed in efforts to control the nationalistic movement, and their effects are evident in indicators of public disorder.

Definitions, Crime, and Strife (b_1)

It is problematic whether changes in legal definition alone can change the patterns of social disorder, either "crime" or strife. Legal changes are supposed to depend for any deterrent effect they may have on the threat, and occasional actuality, of punishment. The case for a linkage of the sort represented in Figure II.6.1 by arrow b_1 rests on evidence that in some societies, for many citizens, "the law" has a moral force sufficient to ensure that legal change brought about by legitimate authorities using legitimate procedures will discourage newly criminalized behavior. Direct evidence for this is very difficult to come by, but New South Wales affords one dramatic example. When legislation enacted during World War I made the International Workers of the World an illegal organization, its leaders suspended activities and presented themselves for arrest. The validity of the example is suspect, however, because the behavior was probably motivated as much by bravado as by acceptance of the legitimacy of the new law.

The extent of threatening social behavior affects legal definitions in more visible ways. As suggested previously, an increase in some kinds of strife or deviance increases public concern, giving rise in turn to elite or popular demands for legal redefinition. It is also possible that a decline in the sense of concern about particular kinds of behavior paves the way for their decriminalization, but there are relatively few examples of formal decriminalization in the four societies we have studied. One is the decriminalization of homosexuality in England during the 1960s; another is the Swedish relaxation of legal restraints on abortion. In both instances, however, it was not behavior that changed but prevailing notions of what behavior was acceptable, or anyway tolerable enough not to require public control.

Still another way in which the extent of crime and strife can affect legal definitions is illustrated by the "decriminalization" of labor organizations and strike activity, a process that occurred in all four societies, albeit at different times and in different circumstances. As the industrial labor force grew in size so did labor organizing and strike activity, despite vigorous and sporadically effective official efforts at suppression. Generally the workers redoubled their efforts with some redirection to political activity; as a result, efforts at control became too costly and in some instances downright impossible to continue. In terms of our model, the outcome in these societies was a redefinition of public disorder in norms and in formal-legal terms: Workers gained enough influence to ensure that most activities of organized labor became politically tolerable, whereupon the legal regulation of the activities in question was markedly relaxed. In the three Western societies the process involved no abrupt, fundamental political upheaval; in India workers were among the vanguard of the revolutionary movement that overturned, not the rules of the game, but the players.

In the examples just cited the effects of social disorder on legal definitions are mediated by political factors, notably the scope of public concern about what constitutes unacceptable individual and collective behavior. Is this principle general enough to be made a theoretical assumption? We symbolize our belief that this is true by showing no direct link in Figure II.6.1 between the extent of social disorder on the one hand and legal definitions on the other. This is not a trivial assumption: It directs attention to the diverse political processes that intervene between changes in "disorderly" behavior and formal-legal specification of the behaviors that deserve public control.

Police, Punishment, and Public Disorder (d_1, d_2)

Police systems vary in their primary objective: They may be mainly concerned with controlling civil strife (as in Calcutta throughout the twentieth century), or with protecting a ruling class, rather than preventing and detecting individual crime—which is the conventional task of contemporary police. Whatever their principal tasks, police systems can be more or less comprehensive and efficient, and more or less self-serving, in detecting and recording illegal acts and in arresting suspects. How thoroughly they keep records and perform their duties is directly reflected in crime statistics, which provide our main indicators of "public disorder." Police efficiency is less directly reflected in the extent of public concern about crime. Victimization surveys and everyday observation demonstrate that a large volume of illegal behavior goes undetected, or at least unreported, in contemporary societies. This reservoir is an ever-present potential for "crime waves" arising from increased reporting by the public (linkage d_2) or from increased efforts at detection and apprehension by the police (linkage d_1). The publicity given "crime waves" has been a major reinforcement for public alarm about disorder in Western societies throughout this century, not merely in the last 25 years, and some of these phenomena have been much more a function of police action and journalistic incitement than of changes in social behavior. Examples involving crimes against sexual morality are particularly numerous. A case in point was a fivefold increase in arrest rates for prostitution offenses in New South Wales between 1958 and the early 1960s, followed by an equally precipitous decline, apparently due to a police crackdown preceded by considerable expression of moral opposition. The other side of the coin is represented by an abrupt temporary decline in arrests for soliciting in London in the early 1920s. Police made a particularly ill-advised arrest, creating such a public furor that some magistrates refused to convict and police enforcement was temporarily suspended.

The connections between police and judicial policies and public disorder can be even more complex. Growth in public concern about disorder often may stimulate more rigorous enforcement and lead to changes in the way the courts carry out business: Accused offenders may face greater likelihood of being found guilty and may receive sentences longer than heretofore given. In the history of New South Wales, for example, the following sequence of events is repeatedly observed. First is an increase in public concern, stimulated by the fulminations of clergymen, journalists, and/or citizens' action groups, about some dramatic type of crime—bushranging, Chinese opium dens, razor gangs, abortion, pack-rape, or what have you. One or a handful of publicized instances of the crime usually suffices to generate the wave of concern. What follows is a flurry of official pronouncements and legislative activity, prescribing heavy penalties for the crime, now more precisely defined, and also intensified police activity and the imposition of harsh sentences on offenders. Public concern soon subsides, usually paralleling a drop in the incidence of reported offenses as the police relax their vigilance; still later the courts begin to hand down less severe sentences.

A feature of these episodes of public disorder that bears special mention is the "placebo effect" of changing police and· judicial policies in response to rising public disorder. Irrespective of whether or not the new policies affect social behavior—which is generally unknown anyway—"crackdowns" often are intrinsically satisfying to those who raised the alarm. Such episodes also furnish a rationale for increasing the resources of police and judicial systems. On a number of occasions, in all the four cities, increases in public disorder led to strengthening and reorganization of police forces. This is not a general warrant for a cynical "theory" to the effect that crime waves are generated by the police for self-serving purposes, but there is no doubt that crime reports and the sense of public disorder about both crime and strife are sometimes manipulated by officials and political groups to justify particular judicial and police policies. In a recent study of urban American crime rates, for example, Seidman and

Couzens demonstrate that rates of serious property crime in 1970-1971 were systematically deflated in eight of 30 cities by undervaluing larcenies; in the case of Washington, D.C., the "results" were used to demonstrate the "success" of the federal government's new anticrime program.[11]

Public Policies and Behavioral Control (e_1, e_2)

The last linkages in this part of the model are the connections between police and judicial policies and the objective extent of threatening social behavior. It is a token of popular and official belief that certain public order policies reduce crime and strife and others do not. Linkage e_2 symbolizes these multifarious connections. Neither officials, academics, politicos, nor ordinary citizens agree on which policies have which effect, but all believe that something works. It is likely that the more certain is punishment for crime, the lower is the "true" incidence of criminal behavior; and if certainty is fairly high, the more severe the punishment, the greater the deterrent effect. This equation does not necessarily hold for civil strife, however. The frequent escalation of demonstrations and strikes into violent confrontations in response to police intervention suggests what can happen on a small scale; the history of the nationalist movement in Bengal illustrates the point on a grand scale. The effectiveness of policies of public order for controlling strife rests more on dissuading potential participants than on punishing activists. If the participants are sufficiently numerous and serious, the existing institutions of public order can almost always be overwhelmed.

The hypothetical effects of punishment on crime cannot readily be demonstrated in the cities we studied because ordinarily the certainty of detection and arrest, and the likelihood of subsequent punishment, were too low to make much difference for the more common crimes—especially theft and "crimes against morality and custom." No doubt that is a principal reason for their commonness: Only by a massive and sustained investment in "order maintenance" and a Stalinist disregard for due process could the police and courts alone reduce substantially the incidence of the more frequently committed crimes. As a rule the intense efforts required to raise the risks of crime are devoted to offenses that are socially and politically most threatening—murder, kidnapping, terrorism, and a few others.

The new policies and reformed institutions of public order in the three Western cities in the nineteenth century apparently reduced the incidence of crime. We hypothesize that this occurred because policies and institutions were linked, by accident or design, with social changes that eroded the conditions responsible for threatening behavior. For example, the incidence of property crime in London in the second quarter of the nineteenth century was extraordinarily high. Much of it was perpetrated by homeless youths now labeled "delinquents." Those who survived the rigors of street life and numerous brief stays in poisonously unhealthy prisons graduated into the "criminal class" of adults, who were both victims and agents of much other social nastiness. Midcentury, however, brought the establishment of a system of reformatory and industrial schools where youthful offenders were confined for long periods, fed regularly, and given rudimentary training. This shift in penal practices coincided with a long-term expansion of economic opportunities; the two together appear to have been a major cause of the significant decline in theft that began in the 1850s and the eventual diminution of the distinctive "criminal class."

The general principle proposed here is that the policies followed by the police, judicial, and penal institutions have their intended effects on criminal behavior only in limited social circumstances. Once those rather narrow limits are exceeded, by larger cultural, socioeconomic, or political changes, established policies of public order have less and less effect and ultimately may be self-defeating. This brings us to the causal linkage labeled e_1 in Figure II.6.1: the direct effects of social disorder on police and judicial systems and policies. An answer for strife has already been suggested: If it is sufficiently intense, widespread, and prolonged, it can overwhelm the institutions of public order. This is seemingly what happened in Bengal. The burgeoning nationalism of 1910-1946 eroded the capacity of the police and courts to deal with ordinary crime and ultimately their capacity to do anything at all, as long as they remained under British control. A sustained increase in serious "crime" is likely to have comparable effects. As it increases, conventional efforts at control are likely to be increased; insofar as they fail to work, the police and courts will put heavier emphasis on ritualistic responses and institutional self-preservation. Reform and renovation are not ruled out, but to be effective they need to be consonant with whatever changing social circumstances are responsible for the changes in patterns of behavior.

The immediate conditions of public disorder are so interdependent that it is difficult indeed to understand one without describing the others. And that is one of the points of the discussion just concluded. The causal connections among the conditions of public order can be neatly summarized in a model such as Figure II.6.1, but that is no license for studying any one of them in isolation. It also bears repeating that this model is not explicit enough to be a "theory" of public disorder. Few hypotheses have spelled out precise connections among any of these conditions. Each refers not to one but a whole set of variables. Public disorder has several aspects, for example, and the efforts and effects of police and judicial systems comprise many characteristics. Formal theory would require that each be separately defined and linked by assumption or hypothesis with the others. It is too soon for this kind of detailed conceptualization. The general suggestion is that such connections are plausible and merit more careful empirical study and theoretical specification. Our city studies are a contribution to the first of these tasks.

THE INDIRECT CONDITIONS OF PUBLIC DISORDER

Time and again the discussion just concluded refers to factors like elites' interests and socioeconomic conditions that alter one or another of the immediate conditions of public disorder. The theories about the causes of "crime" and civil conflict, reviewed earlier, include much longer lists of social conditions thought to affect disorder, directly or indirectly. We now ask how we can think about and organize information on these conditions and their effects.[12]

The "exogenous" influences on public disorder are of three general types, here labeled "elite goals," "economic imperatives," and "social scale and cultural heterogeneity." The goals and interests of the political elite shape legal definitions of disorder and the nature of official responses to it. The structure and requirements of the eco-

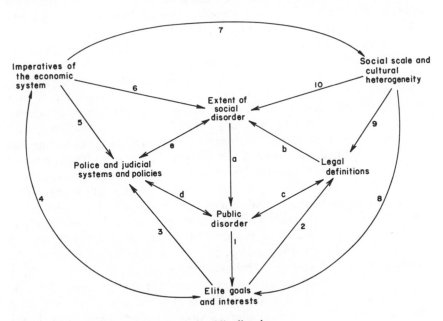

Figure II.6.2 The indirect conditions of public disorder

nomic system influence the goals of the elite and limit the resources members of the elite can give to order maintenance. Far from least, much of the civil strife and some "crime" in contemporary societies flows from the onerous requirements of systems of production and the unequal distribution of their products. Social scale and cultural heterogeneity are also implicated as causes of disorder, according to some of the criminogenic and conflict theories already reviewed, as well as being interdependent with elite goals and economic imperatives. Proposals about the relations among these variables, and their effects on public disorder, can be discussed in relation to the schematization of Figure II.6.2.

Goals and Interests of the Political Elite

Insofar as political elites are directly threatened by social disorder (linkage 1 of Figure II.6.2), they are almost certain to attempt to control it by whatever means come to hand (linkages 2 and 3). If their personal property and safety are at risk, one can expect that at a minimum they will establish safeguards for themselves. If their position and perquisites are threatened by the collective action of other groups, those actions too will be restrained by any legal and institutional means available. The same two principles apply to non-elites, but these groups are not always able to give their views the force of law and the weight of official sanction. Insofar as non-elites are politically influential, their goals and interests are also directly relevant to the shaping of laws and policies of public order.

Elites have objectives and face problems other than those of maintaining their conception of public order. If their primary objective is to impose a particular moral or political orthodoxy on society, they will take one tack in defining and controlling disorder; if they are mainly concerned with such goals as economic growth, international conquest, or simply maintaining their own perquisites, they will take quite a different approach. There also are great differences in elites' assumptions about the appropriateness and effectiveness of different means for maintaining order—however that term is defined. Elites' views are vital on questions such as the following: What categories or modes of social activity are most valued and disvalued? How humanely or callously ought people to treat one another? Where does the locus of responsibility for deviance fall—on the individual, on his primary group, or on society at large? What are the relative merits of negative and positive sanctions as means of influencing behavior? Of course other groups in society have views on such questions, but it is the political elite whose norms are most directly translated into policies of public order. Thus there is virtually always an elite "tilt" to the laws and policies of public order, and the significant question is not "whether" but "how much."

The views of elites about the means and ends of social action are influenced by general economic and social considerations. They also are subject to modification as social and public circumstances change. An increase in the actual incidence of crime or strife is likely to increase the salience of order maintenance for the elite, and in any quasi-open political system, a rise in popular concern about disorder will likely have the same effect. The hypothesis can be stated explicitly: As official indicators of social disorder rise, the relative importance of order maintenance among elite goals also tends to rise. It is more doubtful whether there is a reverse process, whereby elites turn attention and resources away from order maintenance once their version of "order" has improved. Those who define and police public order can take advantage of numerous means of "creating" disorder. This possibility, combined with the tendency of specialized bureaucracies to perpetuate themselves, suggests that the institutions of public order are more readily expanded than contracted. The three Western cities treated here furnish ample evidence: Despite their common, long-term experience of declining common crimes from the mid-nineteenth century to the 1920s, their police forces continued to expand (commensurate with population) and to modernize. The scope of criminal law also was extended: A great deal of legislation was passed, defining and proscribing new kinds of offenses against sexual morality and public order especially. Such evidence is not definitive, of course, because these trends are backed by other factors as well—significantly, the functional necessity of regulating the increased traffic and commercial activities of growing cities.

Imperatives of the Economic System

The basis and structure of a society's system of production will directly or indirectly affect all other conditions of public disorder. First and most fundamentally, economic and ecological factors impose serious limits on the kinds of goals that can be pursued by elites (Figure II.6.2, linkage 4). They also constrain the kinds of institutions that can be maintained, including but not restricted to the institutions of public order (linkage 5). To take an extreme case, a society that produces only enough for bare subsistence of its members has no "surplus product" to support a specially privileged elite, much less to create specialized institutions of order maintenance. Highly productive capitalist and socialist societies enjoy a broader range of alternatives, but even Lyndon Johnson's "Great Society" of the late 1960s was unable to support both war and welfare. Moreover *any* division of labor and *any* pattern of distribution of goods create some kind of potential for conflict and social deviance (linkage 6). Division of labor creates differences of interest, over which groups will clash; and both produce a need for hierarchic control and coordination, which is always to some degree resented and resisted by those who are controlled.[13] Individually, men almost always aspire to more than they have, even when everyone has the same; and some in every society are driven or tempted to use "deviant" means to satisfy their aspirations.[14] Different modes of production and patterns of distribution generate different types and degrees of social disorder, but neither feudalism nor capitalism nor socialism nor utopian communism can be free of such dissonance.[15]

Certain kinds of connections are expected to exist between economic structures and the public order policies formulated by elites (linkage 4). For example, water diversion will be as heinous a crime in a hydraulic society as cattle theft is in a herding economy. If the economic system depends on the accumulation of material goods—whether for consumption or for capital investment—legal codes and public order policies will give especially close attention to crimes of acquisition. Civil strife involving workers will be of intense concern in economies that depend on large, docile supplies of cheap labor. Economic structures also will affect the specific institutions and policies chosen (linkage 5). The kinds of police systems established to carry out public order policies will be quite directly affected by a society's surplus product: Poor societies are likely to have small and weak police systems; the rich can devote large resources to the maintenance of public order. Thus a high level of public order may be a kind of social luxury, one that becomes a matter of elite concern only when surplus means for its attainment become available. Ways of treating offenders also are influenced by a society's modes of production and its fiscal status. Wealthy societies can afford to imprison and resocialize offenders; corporal punishment is more economically feasible for poor societies. And in societies where labor is scarce, or especially unpleasant economic tasks have to be performed, it is more likely that offenders will be put to forced labor than imprisoned or executed. Wealthy as the three Western societies in this study are, the evidence is that their elites at present would rather release offenders than invest additional resources in imprisonment or rehabilitation.

The characteristics of civil strife also are affected by modes of production, in at least three general ways (linkage 6). In any economic system that relies on a division of labor and authority, workers recurrently resist and contest the conditions of their servitude or employment. In slaveholding societies revolt was a dreaded occurrence, and feudal overlords faced always the threat of peasant rebellions. Colonial rulers and entrepreneurs must anticipate revolts, wars of independence, and crises of nationalization arising out of the ever-present resentment of indigenous clients and workers to the export of the fruits of their labor. Modern capitalists and managers of socialist economies are obliged to deal repeatedly with strikes, slowdowns, sabotage, and certainly in the United States and Britain, chronic theft by employees. These kinds of disorder are manifestations of "business as usual" in their respective economic systems. They are distinct from the exceptional episodes of resistance and rebellion by workers that accompany transformations from one type of economic system to another. Familiar examples of the latter in the Western historical experience are laborers' resistance to new economic arrangements, such as the English peasants who opposed the enclosure acts and, later, the machine-breaking Luddites, as well as the growing numbers of wage-earning laborers who struggled to gain economic bargaining rights and political suffrage. The third kind of economic-based conflict also occurs as a consequence of fundamental economic change, when rising economic classes—whether new feudal landowners, an urban bourgeoisie, or a new managerial elite— challenge the old political elite. Such challenges may be resolved by co-optation and accommodation, or by revolution.

Economic conditions, as distinct from economic structures, also have certain immediate effects on types and incidence of crime. Economic stress—declining productivity, rising unemployment—often is cited as a source of increased property crime and, depending on the society, as a cause of banditry, bread riots, or strikes. A second line of argument, which on its face is contradictory, is that increases in a society's wealth serve to increase the absolute and relative frequency of occurrence of property crime. There are two versions of the argument. One is that the affluence of rising classes inspires envy and deprivation in the less fortunate, who respond by taking what comes to hand. The other is simply that there is more to be stolen in affluent societies. The evidence of the city studies is that poverty *and* wealth are correlated with the incidence of common crime, not only theft but crimes against the person as well. In nineteenth century London, Stockholm, and New South Wales both theft and assault increased during periods of economic slump and declined when economic conditions improved again. Economic distress had very little effect on crime rates in either direction in the twentieth century, but as total productivity (wealth) increased, so did common crime. Evidently two separate causal processes were at work at different times. We can only speculate about whether the difference is due to the effects of a third variable or to a shift in the direction of social causality above some threshold in affluence.[16]

Social Scale and Cultural Heterogeneity

The economic structure of a society exerts a marked influence on the numbers and distribution of its population, the size and functions of its settlements, the diversity of interests among its members, the nature of social relations among individuals and groups, and the scope and complexity of its noneconomic institutions—in other words, almost everything (Figure II.6.2, linkage 7). But it does not precisely determine these conditions. The scale and complexity of a society, and the extent to which it is comprised of diverse cultural groups, have important and independent effects on the conditions of public disorder. Two general kinds of connections of this kind are included in our model. The first is that social and cultural factors influence elite goals and interests (linkage 8). The priorities and preferred means of the elites will reflect the values and norms of the cultural groups from which they come; and their policies toward public order will vary depending on the extent of cultural heterogeneity. Socially heterogenous societies are characterized by two different approaches to public order. One defines the common public order narrowly and practices compromise and accommodation when formulating common laws and policies. The other imposes uniformity through coercive control of "deviant" cultural groups. The significance of social scale is that large and complex societies have much greater problems of public order than small and simple ones, because there are so many more people and activities to be coordinated and regulated. Large size and complexity cannot be maintained in a society unless these functional requirements are met.

Much evidence and theoretical speculation links social scale and cultural heterogeneity to the definition and extent of disorder (linkages 9 and 10). One general kind of argument is that the larger and more diverse a community, the less effective are informal, face-to-face methods of controlling and punishing deviance. Thus as cities and societies grow, the likelihood increases that the elites will find it necessary to define and proscribe unacceptable behavior, and the more likely they will be to rely on specialized institutions to maintain order. Moreover, as communities expand and become varied—conditions that usually follow on increasing specialization in economic activities—human interactions tend to become more complex and diverse, hence unpredictable. The typical, probably essential response of elites is to tighten legal definitions of acceptable behavior and to police such activities more carefully. A distinct trend in the four societies we studied here is the veritable explosion of laws and administrative codes designed to regulate day-to-day interactions, in domains as dissimilar as trade, public demeanor, and traffic.

One class of hypotheses especially relevant to social order in cities specifies ways in which increases in urban population and heterogeneity generate increased crime and strife (linkage 10). Four of the possible reasons are as follows.

1. Increasing cultural heterogeneity provides more varied standards of behavior, leading to erosion of the normative standards of behavior of the dominant social groups, hence fewer internal inhibitions to deviant behavior.

2. Increasing concentration of population leads to overcrowding, whose consequences may include physiological reactions that increase aggressiveness, or more social occasions for hostile interactions.

3. Increasing concentration of population contributes to "dehumanization" and anonymity of human relationships; the first of which helps justify aggressive and exploitative treatment of others, while the second makes it easier to get away with doing so.

4. Increasing size and heterogeneity together increase intergroup friction and provide more occasions for friction, which can lead to individual and collective attacks on members of opposing groups.

Still other paths from social scale and cultural heterogeneity to social disorder are mapped by the theories of crime and strife reviewed earlier. Cultural differentiation and conflict are important elements in Nettler's four types of criminogenic theories, and in all but the purely psychological kinds of explanations proposed for civil strife. This is not to claim that the concept of "social scale and cultural heterogeneity" comprises all the causal variables cited in explanations of crime and strife. It is possible, though, to map almost all the general socioeconomic and political conditions thought to affect social disorder onto the network of variables depicted in Figure II.6.2. Those which are not aspects of scale and heterogeneity can be treated as aspects or consequences of the economic system, or of elite interests. Finally, most of the proposed psychosocial mechanisms by which social conditions are translated into "disorderly" behavior are consistent with the justifications offered previously for the connections indicated among the variables in the model.

The usefulness of the framework proposed here does not depend on its consistency with other theories: It has the similarities to others' arguments because some other theories have been incorporated into this larger framework. Its value depends on whether it facilitates further research on the nature and sources of public disorder. What it should do, and what it has done in this study, is to call attention to kinds of information not previously considered in this context, and to suggest new questions for precise theoretical treatment.

ON THE DECAY AND DISSOLUTION OF SOCIAL SYSTEMS

Social disorder, if sufficiently intense and prolonged, destroys social systems. A condition in which all are at war is a philosophical, empirical, and political definition of the absence of a social system. In developing the framework little has been said about the circumstances under which social systems can self-destruct. Some very tentative answers can be drawn out of the model, however, and two are mentioned briefly here. First, there is potential for "positive feedback" among the immediate conditions of public disorder (linkages a to e, Figure II.6.2). That is, some kinds of policies of public order can have effects opposite from those intended for them; namely, they can increase rather than decrease social and public disorder. This is not only a theoretical possibility but one for which specific empirical examples can be extracted from the city studies, especially Calcutta. Second, positive feedback may develop among elements of the economic and social system and the extent of social disorder (linkages 6, 7, and 10). The expansion of economic systems tends to increase social scale and cultural diversity, which in turn can act to increase social disorder in a number of ways already suggested. Beyond some threshold, social disorder will undermine the economic system—directly by reducing the efficiency of production, indirectly by increasing the proportion of resources that must be drained off into order-maintenance activities.

Political elites play a crucial coordinating role in these processes; depending on their goals and their understanding of social causality, they may or may not be able and willing to make requisite adjustments in the economic system and policies of public order. Revolution is likely to ensue in the absence of such adjustments; yet revolution is no sure cure for social dissolution, since there is no guarantee that revolutionaries or anybody else possess the means and will to reconstruct a complex and orderly society. There has been no dramatic disintegration of social systems in recent Western history, which no doubt has reinforced the optimism about "social development" typical of Marxist and liberal scholars and ideologists alike. There are enough historical and non-Western examples, though, to suggest that theories founded on premises of irreversible social evolution are incomplete and suspect.

AN EPILOGUE ON POLICIES FOR PUBLIC ORDER

It is understandable if the reader, having journeyed through a dense thicket of facts, figures, and concepts about public order, feels dissatisfied that no formula or strategy has been offered by which public order might be improved in our time. The first antidote is the reminder that none was promised. Second, we note that the investigations of the four cities reveal a great diversity of policies that seemed at various times to improve public order; other policies whose effects left much to be desired are also identified. The more problematic question is whether the improvements that occurred, especially between 1850 and 1930, were due to the policies of public order themselves or to their coincidence with more fundamental cultural, economic, and political changes. The disquieting general conclusion of this study about "policies of public order" is that the effects of these policies depend on other circumstances, only dimly understood.

As a result there is little empirical basis for confidence about the contemporary effects of policies informed by humanitarian faith in equalization of opportunity and rehabilitation, or by conservative reliance on strict authority and firm punishment. It *may* be true that the reduction of urban poverty, the decriminalization of social offenses, and the creation of across-the-board programs of rehabilitation and social reintegration for offenders would turn back the surge in common crime that has marked the second half of this century. It *may* be true that systematic application by modern police and courts of the horrendous penalties prescribed 200 years ago would virtually eliminate common crime and civil strife—yet it is highly unlikely that such policies will be instituted in any Western society as now constituted. Since liberal reforms have always been resisted by substantial social groups on grounds of principle and economic self-interest, most implementations have been grudging and partial. Worse yet, the reformist principles are rapidly being discredited by their apparent failure to check rising disorder. On the other hand people today lack the callous acceptance of brutality that would be needed to administer the traditional solutions, and even if officials could be found to implement them, the policies in their pure form are utterly unacceptable to large segments of contemporary political and social opinion. If applied they would engender not order but disorder, in the form of resistance to oppression. Thus the possibilities for devising effective and broadly supported policies of public order are constrained by the same diversity of beliefs and purposes that becomes manifest in increased disorder. The people of Western societies simply are not of one mind about the most desirable behavioral standards or policies of social control.

The problem, and the inherent difficulty of solving it in modern democratic societies, can be put another way. The fundamental precondition for public order is congruence between the cultural values of the ordinary members of a society and the operating codes of order and opportunity maintained by political elites. Where common values and ruling codes diverge, for whatever reasons, disorder increases; and as they converge, order increases. Pressures for divergence, which arise from the inherently dissimilar interests of rulers and ruled, grow stronger as societies increase in complexity. Convergence, and a modicum of social order, are rare in complex societies. Where it is found, convergence is more likely to be the result of long-term social engineering, consistently applied, than the workings of natural social forces. The processes of "social engineering" are manipulative and often oppressive, a circumstance that raises a fundamental question: Are the costs of social disorder more bearable than the costs of order? This question has no empirical answer. For the time being, however, most of the citizens of three Western societies seem to be prepared to accept the costs of disorder; the citizens of West Bengal have little choice in the matter.

NOTES TO PART II, CHAPTER 6

1. In the remainder of this chapter "crime" in quotation marks refers to threatening individual behavior; when the word crime is used without quotes, the reference is to criminal behavior as legally defined.

2. Nettler, *Explaining Crime.* Another survey of social theories of crime cited earlier is Mannheim, *Comparative Criminology.* For reviews of biological, psychological, and anthropological theories of crime and individual violence see Mannheim, Part 3, and Mulvilhill and Tumin, *Crimes of Violence,* chs. 7-10.

3. Nettler, op. cit., chs. 6-7, quotation pp. 140-141.

4. Ibid., ch. 8, so classifies E. H. Sutherland's "differential association" hypothesis (see E. H. Sutherland and D. R. Cressey, *Criminology,* various eds., Philadelphia: Lippincott) and labeling explanations of criminality, initiated by Howard S. Becker, *Outsiders: Studies in the Sociology of Deviance* (New York:/Free Press, 1963).

5. The principal examples of control theory cited by Nettler (op. cit., ch. 9) are the "containment" theory proposed by W. C. Reckless in *The Crime Problem,* various eds. (New York: Appleton-Century-Crofts) and the analyses of defective social training by H. J. Eysenck, *Crime and Personality* (Boston: Houghton Mifflin, 1964) and G. Trasler, *The Explanation of Criminality* (London: Routledge and Kegan Paul, 1962).

6. This discussion follows the more detailed comparisons of theoretical approaches in T. R. Gurr, "The Revolution-Social-Change Nexus, Some Old Theories and New Hypotheses," *Comparative Politics,* (April 1973), 363-378. Examples of psychological approaches to the explanation of civil strife include E. Victor Wolfenstein, *The Revolutionary Personality: Lenin, Trotsky, Gandhi* (Princeton, N.J.: Princeton University Press, 1967) and David C. Schwartz, *Political Alienation and Political Behavior* (Chicago: Aldine-Atherton, 1973).

7. Three similar sociopsychological theories are James C. Davies, "Toward a Theory of Revolution," *American Sociological Review,* 27 (February, 1962), 5-19; Ivo K. Feierabend, Rosalind L. Feierabend, and Betty A. Nesvold, "Social Change and Political Violence: Cross-National Comparisons," in Hugh Davis Graham and T. R. Gurr, eds., *Violence in America,* and T. R. Gurr, *Why Men Rebel.*

8. Two influential theories emphasizing aspects of social structure are Neil J. Smelser, *Theory of Collective Behavior* (New York: Free Press, 1963) and Chalmers Johnson, *Revolutionary Change* (Boston: Little, Brown, 1966).

9. Aristotle developed a group conflict theory of political change in *The Politics,* Book V. The best-known contemporary theories of class conflict derive from Karl Marx's writings. Two influential non-Marxist theories are Johan Galtung, "A Structural Theory of Aggression," *Journal of Peace Research* (No. 2, 1964), 95-119, which parallels the Aristotelian argument, and Dahrendorf, *Class and Class Conflict in Industrial Society,* which is concerned with the sources and consequences of group conflict generally.

10. This and subsequent examples are illustrative, not definitive.

11. David Seidman and Michael Couzens, "Getting the Crime Rate Down: Political Pressure and Crime Reporting," *Law and Society* (Spring 1974), 457-493. Specifically, the evidence is that the District of Columbia police, and

apparently those of at least seven other large cities, began in the late 1960s or 1970 to value a significantly larger portion of larcencies at "under $50" and a smaller portion at "over $50." The total number of crimes is not affected, but the number of "serious" crimes declines as a consequence—and the latter are included in the summary Index of the FBI's Uniform Crime Reporting System. Such a change enabled the police commissioner of Baltimore to claim a 15.1 percent decline in major crime during the first half of 1971 by comparison with the first half of 1970 (cited in Seidman and Couzens, 480).

12. In the terms used to describe formal models in econometrics, the four variables shown in Figure II.6.1 are "endogenous," and the relationships shown among them are too numerous for the equations expressing them to be identified. The additional variables shown in Figure II.6.2 and discussed below are "exogenous." Of course any discussion of the formal status of such a model is premature because the variable aspects of most of the conditions are not specified here, and indices are not suggested for most of them.

13. Similar arguments, developed in more detail, include Dahrendorf, op. cit.; Harry Eckstein and T. R. Gurr, *Patterns of Authority: A Structural Basis for Political Inquiry* (New York: Wiley, 1975), chs. 15 and 16; and Arnold Feldman, "Violence and Volatility: The Likelihood of Revolution," in Harry Eckstein, ed., *Internal War: Problems and Approaches* (New York: Free Press, 1963).

14. For a formal, deductive theory about relations between actors' attainments and their expectations, and the consequences of different patterns of distribution for their potential for conflict behavior, see T. R. Gurr and Raymond Duvall, *Conflict and Society: A Formal Theory and Contemporary Evidence* (forthcoming), Part I.

15. The Marxian emphasis on the fundamental importance of a society's economic system in accounting for its other characteristics is accepted here, but not Marx's precise determinism: Economic factors limit the range of societal and political variation but do not exactly determine the shape of institutions and interests. The position here is that all conceivable economic structures create "antagonisms" that constitute a potential for social disorder.

16. Other studies also show evidence of an apparent reversal in causality. When compared with economic data, national crime data for the United States, Canada, England and Wales, and Scotland from 1900 to 1970 show positive correlations between unemployment and crime before World War II, and positive correlations between economic growth and crime thereafter. M. Harvey Brenner, "Effects of the Economy on Criminal Behavior and the Administration of Criminal Justice: A Multinational Study," paper presented to the Conference on Economic Crisis and Crime, United Nations Social Defence Research Institute, Rome, 1975. The results are more complex than this summary suggests, and Brenner puts a somewhat different interpretation on them.